S0-ARK-178

THE MASTER KEY OF WISDOM

VOLUME I
Know Yourself the Chung Doe Way

CHARLES WON-SUK KIM

authorHOUSE™

1663 LIBERTY DRIVE, SUITE 200
BLOOMINGTON, INDIANA 47403
(800) 839-8640
WWW.AUTHORHOUSE.COM

AuthorHouse™
1663 Liberty Drive, Suite 200
Bloomington, IN 47403
www.authorhouse.com
Phone: 1-800-839-8640

AuthorHouse™ UK Ltd.
500 Avebury Boulevard
Central Milton Keynes, MK9 2BE
www.authorhouse.co.uk
Phone: 08001974150

Key words: 1. Philosophy 2. Martial Arts 3. Chi Energy 4. Self-improvement 5. Leadership 6. Mentorship 7. Moo Doe 8. Wisdom

© 2007 Charles Won-suk Kim and Grandmaster Iron Kim.
  All rights reserved.

No part of this book may be reproduced, stored in
a retrieval system, or transmitted by any means
without the written permission of the author.

First published by AuthorHouse 5/16/2007

ISBN: 978-1-4259-9561-4 (e)
ISBN: 978-1-4259-9355-9 (sc)

Library of Congress Control Number: 2007901282

Printed in the United States of America
Bloomington, Indiana

This book is printed on acid-free paper.

To Jeane and Jenelle, and to Judy, Richard and Peter, for the best of their interpretation, for not losing the meaning of the principles in this book, for their help in teaching instructors, students and the readers to find the correct path to inner peace and happiness.

Contents

FOREWORD

THIS IS THE TRUE LEGEND OF Grandmaster Borion, Grandmaster "Iron" Kim's master. This book is based on a true story and the first presentation in English of Moo Doe moral principles by a Moo Doe grandmaster. In *The Master Key of Wisdom: Volume I*, Grandmaster Kim reveals in compelling simplicity the range, scope, and key elements of the moral system handed down over many centuries of time from one grandmaster to the next as a pattern for daily living. Grandmaster Kim made the determination late in 1999 to provide this moral road-map as a guide and "master key" for all those who are embracing Moo Doe practices with a serious commitment to personal challenge. The objective is to learn and to practice Moo Doe wisdom to bring about a significant increase in balance, harmony, integrity, security, peace, joy, love, and wellness for a brighter future.

The lessons are given in each chapter to easily understand your inner self, and provides enduring solutions from the Chung Doe (correct path) principle to improve yourself. This book sets forth a way for any human being who will carefully follow the eight-step formula of *The Master Key of Wisdom* to cultivate a rich and abundant increase in that all-too rare virtue—wisdom.

This is a grand step forward in cultivating and leaving behind the good seeds of harmony, peace, and joy for your family and friends. Every reader is urged to carefully study the dialogues, lessons, and engage in supplementary exercises of each chapter and to make this material an enduring part of his or her life.

The Master Key of Wisdom is a path that leads to good principle, where you can have security with peace in your life. It is a goal many human beings are searching for and one of the best ways to achieve success, leaving behind a meaningful legacy for the coming generations.

Because this book is geared toward the student of Moo Doe, there are several East Asian terms and concepts that are translated into English. It is inevitable that words in one language translated to another, especially conceptual terms, are difficult to retain exact meaning. The terms throughout become clear as the reader progresses through the book. We have, however, included a glossary for clarity.

BASED ON TRUE STORIES

This book is based on Grandmaster "Iron" Kim's memories of his master, Grandmaster Borion. The author takes you along the journey of Grandmaster "Iron" Kim, who began his learning as a young boy in an Am Ja, which is a secluded place of meditation for enlightenment in the mountains of East Asia. During that time, the young boy experienced some of the difficult challenges of life and attained knowledge to understand the wisdom of life. At this young age, Grandmaster Borion taught him the basic Three Steps of Enlightenment. The first step is to understand yourself, both mind and body, in order to purify yourself and know your skills and abilities. The second step is to understand others' minds and bodies and know their abilities. The third step is to purify your soul in order to open your heart and connect with your universal spirit, enabling you to reach the ultimate goal of enlightenment.

There are seven steps that are the foundation to reach a higher spiritual level. Once these steps are completed, it is your choice to continue learning the eighth and higher steps for the higher spiritual levels. To become a Moo Doe master, it is necessary to learn and absorb this higher spiritual level. It is your desire and ability that will allow you to reach a higher spiritual level. By following the principles of these eight steps, certain human beings have achieved a higher spiritual level of enlightenment, the level of Doe-sa, or the higher level of spiritual teacher.

As a young boy, Grandmaster "Iron" Kim was asked by his master to write a figure eight in the sand with his finger. While his master explained how life is like the figure eight, he began to understand the principle of life. There is harmony and balance in life--there are ups and there are downs. The principles of Chung Doe (the correct way) will give you the correct path to follow in your life. When you follow the correct principles in life, others will respect you and will seek to learn your wisdom and way. However, while you gain more respect, there will be more challenges. You must remember that taller mountains are always hit by stronger winds.

Regardless of the positive and negative circumstances that will occur during your lifetime, follow the principles of Chung Doe. Then, no matter where you are or where you go, you will always have inner peace. You will have the master key of wisdom.

Now, the wisdom of a traditional Moo Doe grandmaster is shared through generations of Moo Doe masters and centuries of learning so that you can achieve your master key of wisdom. This book was written in the hope of benefiting all human beings.

Charles Won-suk Kim has a doctorate in strategic leadership and has studied Moo Doe principles for over 28 years. A leadership professional for over 18 years, his learning is in both theory and practice from a Traditional Moo Doe grandmaster, as well as formal studies in economics, history, law, management and leadership at Harvard University, Regent University, and Yonsei University (Korea).

According to legend,
the origin of Traditional Moo Doe
comes from the principles of nature,
the principles of Dharma.

One Mind

INTRODUCTION

"TO LIVE IS TO LEARN; TO give is to earn." Each moment of your life is a moment of ultimate choice. Life is a never-ending challenge for good and for bad. Vested in you and each human being is the ability to choose the one or the other.

The good pathway is Chung Doe, leading to greater harmony, balance, integrity, peace, joy, trust, honor, togetherness, and light. Travelers on the Chung Doe pathway have a clear vision of the future. They follow the straight course of principle and honor in their climb toward In Gan, the highest form of humanness. That is the ultimate objective.

The bad pathway is Pa Doe, leading to imbalance, egotism, selfishness, jealousy, anger, alienation, and darkness. Pa Doe travelers circle aimlessly over a fog-shrouded landscape and gradually descend toward Keum

Soo, the wild animal side of humanness, that makes humans behave like beasts. Keum Soo relinquishes principle in favor of Gan Sa, endless flux and superficial change.

Since civilization the law of nature has existed and, for many centuries, masters have taught others and passed down a system of moral principles known as Moo Doe—the master key of wisdom that unlocks the gateway to extraordinary internal and external strengths and the highest level of spirituality. Moo Doe is the road map for accomplishing eight vitally important life goals, which are:

1. Learning to know your "true" self;
2. Making correct daily choices;
3. Overcoming Doe Chi (being drunk with one's (your) own ideas and thoughts);
4. Cultivating good seeds to leave behind for your family;
5. Attaining honor;
6. Changing your reality for the better;
7. Becoming a living vessel of wisdom (being a role model for your family and others); and,
8. Drawing on nature's limitless power through Nae Gong ("wind, fire, and water").

The Moo Doe moral system, in its fullness, is a powerful way to align your destiny and realize your highest potential—physically, mentally, and spiritually. In turn, Moo Doe teaches us to share this light with others.

These eight vital life goals form the heart of *The Master Key of Wisdom*. Each chapter presents a different aspect of the system. The sum total adds up to an infinity of benefits over your lifetime as an active participant, and over the lifetime of your children and the coming generations. Thus the master key is represented by the sign of infinity, displaying the eight symbols of the system.

THE LIVING DIALOGUE

Each of the chapters in *The Master Key of Wisdom* is organized around a dialogue between Grandmaster Borion and his student. You are invited to participate in these short dialogues as the invisible, silent partner. Traditionally, only a select few humans in history have been able to learn directly from a grandmaster. The secrets of Moo Doe were passed down only to humans with the unique capacity and strong character to become grandmasters themselves. Such selectivity applied also to the mysteries of the healing arts that were so effective in preserving a royal line of descent.

Now, as we make the transition into a new century and into a new era where the highest ideals and practices of East and West are flowing together into a greater whole, the time has come to share the Moo Doe teachings with a wider audience. For the first time, this age-old system is being made available to not only in Moo Doe practitioners, but also among the general public. The objective is to extend the healing influence of Moo Doe to practitioners and their families everywhere in order to foster increased well-being and service as part of their daily lives.

For that reason, we encourage you to make the transition within the dialogue format from the role of passive listener to the role of active participant. That is, you are personally invited to take the role of the student and begin to internalize these venerable principles and incorporate them into your own patterns of thought and action.

It is, after all, the internal dialogue within each human being that determines what that human being makes of life. If your internal dialogue is one tending to harmony, balance, peace, joy, and service, then those same outcomes will begin to emerge in your life in greater measure as a living dialogue. In that way, you will begin to cultivate the good seeds to leave behind as a legacy for your own family, as many thousands of humans have already been doing.

The purpose of this book is to foster such a living dialogue within the heart and mind of each participant. Only this kind of pattern of thought and behavior can serve as a strong, solid foundation to better oneself for the next level of training through continuous learning and earning. With this kind of preparation, you can begin to follow the Chung Doe pathway and climb up the Moo Doe mountain toward the fulfillment of your destined potential.

TRANSITION

What follows is the series of eight lessons of Moo Doe morals as taught by Grandmaster Borion. Make this the beginning of your own spiritual journey. The power of Moo Doe originates with the Supreme Being. It is the energy found everywhere in nature that the Moo Doe practitioner, using correct exercises and movements handed down over the centuries, can transform into incredible external and internal strengths. Before you learn these exercises and movements, however, it would be well for you to learn their meaning—the underlying moral principles that will allow you to use these strategies for obtaining the wisdom essential for generating love, harmony, peace, and joy. That is the purpose of *The Master Key of Wisdom*.

Moo Doe is principally a healing power. Everything in nature is made up of energy in one form or another. Through specific exercise and movement techniques (Myung Sang, U Dong Myung Sang, and Nae Gong) proven over centuries, the energy around us can be utilized to enhance vitality and wellness in extraordinary ways. The ancient theory of "wind, fire, and water" comes full circle during the current age of integrative healing when the knowledge of the West is blending with the wisdom of the East for increased benefits to humans everywhere. Our modern modalities of "wind, fire, and water" are the body's magnificent respiratory, thermal, and circulatory systems upon which all health and strength depend. Through the harmony and balance of these systems, life can be lived to the fullest.

This is the moment in history when it is time to reveal many of the Eastern healing secrets for the benefit of all who are willing to learn them and use them for the good of the individual, the family, and the community. Life is a never-ending challenge for good and for bad. Choose the good. Have more balance, more harmony, more joy. Have a longer life, with increased vitality and well-being. Have more togetherness, more service, more happiness, and more spirituality. That is a principle of life. That is the greatest hope for human beings.

THE CIRCLE OF LIFE

It was a joyous reunion when the grandmaster returned from his spiritual journey of several years' duration. To celebrate the occasion, he and his student were climbing together toward the top of a mountain overlooking the valley far below. In the distance, a magnificent temple, perched like a dove on a neighboring summit, reflected back the midday sun. A bell echoed its welcome across the space.

"You have been gone long, Grandmaster. I am glad in my heart that you have returned, " said the student.

The grandmaster smiled and nodded, then said, "Life is a grand journey with many opportunities for spiritual learning and earning. But this latest spiritual journey has taught me lessons as great, perhaps greater."

"You are still learning, Grandmaster?" asked the student in surprise.

"To live is to learn," replied the grandmaster, "and to learn is to earn. Only by living correctly can you learn, and only by sharing with others can you earn the good seeds to pass on to your family and the coming generations."

As he spoke these words, the two travelers reached a spot near a small stream where a grand oak tree offered them respite from the sun.

"Why did you have to remain away so long?" asked the student.

"Life is a challenge for good and for bad," explained the grandmaster. "Some people you meet along the way choose the Chung Doe pathway toward harmony and peace. With the vision of the invisible eye they see the future clearly. Many choose the Pa Doe pathway toward envy and jealousy. They easily lose their way in the fog banks of selfishness and the endless side roads of vain ambition. Chung Doe and Pa Doe—these are opposite ways. The light was always a burden to the darkness. The sun was ever a dispeller of the night. From this come jealousy, greed, and envy. These three companions make foolish decisions that affect not only themselves but their communities as well."

"And you have suffered?" asked the student.

"All learning is suffering," responded the grandmaster, "for in learning we discard the comfortable old self, and exchange it for a self that is wiser and more enlightened. Without pain, there is no rebirth."

Suddenly a gust of wind passed over the mountain ridge and whistled through the branches of the oak tree, which stood unmoved by this natural show of force. Nearby, a small willow tree next to the stream bent pliantly under the force of the wind.

"Look at that willow bush. What do you see?" asked the grandmaster.

"I see a weak little tree that bends and bows under the wind," replied the student.

"While this oak stands strongly in place, you were thinking," added the grandmaster.

"Yes, just like you, Grandmaster," replied the student.

The grandmaster motioned for them to start climbing again and said, "Sometimes strength can be a weakness, and weakness a strength."

"What do you mean?" asked the confused student.

"I recall once a great oak tree near the ocean," continued the grandmaster. "Its character was one of great strength. It stood firm against the fury of a typhoon. The neighboring willow trees flattened themselves against the ground in homage to the ferocious storm. But the oak stood firm and proud in its strength. Then the storm surged in anger and the oak snapped at its base and crashed to the earth. Its strength was its weakness, while the more flexible willow trees lived to see another day."

"Are you saying, Grandmaster, that you have learned something of strength and weakness on your journey?" asked the student.

"Trust is a great strength," replied the grandmaster. "And trust is a great weakness. Trusting the trustworthy is moving with destiny. This trust is invincible and correct. It is an act of honor to honor such trust, once given. But the greedy and the jealous seldom send their icy blasts against such trust and exact a high price in suffering. Thus winners can be losers, and losers winners. How do you see it?"

The student began to deeply ponder and, then, the temple bell sounded in the distance. Suddenly, the student answered, "I believe....that I shall trust in the Supreme Being."

The grandmaster nodded his approval and said, "It is good to place your trust in the Supreme Being. All power, love, and wisdom flow to us from that source, the source of life."

They walked in silence for a few minutes, then the grandmaster said, "Many times during that period I was with you. Did you know this?"

"I felt your presence, Grandmaster, although I did not see you," answered the student.

The grandmaster smiled and said, "Smell the air on this mountain. Take it in. It is part of the abundance of nature too often taken for granted."

"It was because of that life-giving air," continued the grandmaster, "that I learned one of the greatest secrets of life. This secret I now pass on to you."

As the grandmaster spoke these words, the two travelers reached the top of the mountain. On all sides the view was inspiring--to the east, to the west, to the south, to the north.

The grandmaster continued teaching the student and said: "One evening as I was standing breathing in the fresh air from the outside, I discovered new life close to me. A small spider had anchored the beginning of her web line to some stones. She was attempting to span the distance of the rocks. Repeatedly she attempted to leap over this distance, but each time she was repelled by the wind."

"Did she not succeed?" asked the student.

"For many days this battle continued," replied the grandmaster. "The spider was moved by an invincible determination to win. Finally, she succeeded in anchoring the web strand in place, and proceeded to create a web of exceedingly great beauty."

"At last, she could catch her food and eat," said the student.

"Yes," agreed the grandmaster, "the gnats she caught with her web sustained her life just as her drama did mine. Presently she built a large webbed sac into which she deposited the remains of her captives."

"Did she remain inside the sac?" inquired the student.

"No," explained the grandmaster, "she sealed the sac shut and retreated to the lower edge of the web. Then, for the next few days I lost sight of her. I searched for her, but she was gone."

"And the sac?" asked the student.

"The sac came alive," replied the grandmaster. "One morning it opened up and I witnessed a miracle. Many baby spiders emerged to begin their new life. At first they stayed close to the sac. But one day they moved in a line away from the sac and relocated to the lower part of the web. I peered as far down the web as possible. Then the mystery of the missing spider was resolved."

"She was still there?" asked the student with anticipation.

"Yes," replied the grandmaster, "she had anchored herself to the bottom of the web and died. The new young were feeding on her. Her sacrifice was the propagation of her species. She had become the good seed. What greater love is there than that? How do you feel?"

The student swallowed a deep breath of air, sensing that he had just heard something wise. He could think of nothing adequate to say and kept listening.

"That is the circle of life," continued the grandmaster, "from life to death to life. That is the balance of the opposites, the harmony of the differences—Yin and Yang."

The student humbly nodded and lowered his head and said, "I thank you for this wisdom, Grandmaster."

"And I thank the spider," replied the grandmaster.

"How can I learn to be wise like you?" asked the student.

"No matter what happens to you in life, learn from it, and then earn it by sharing with others. If you are in the valley, learn. If you are on the mountain, learn. Then earn. To live is to learn; to give is to earn. You can borrow knowledge from others, but not wisdom. Wisdom you must gain on your own. Just as with life, you gain wisdom by giving it away," replied the grandmaster.

"How can I start to do this, Grandmaster? How can I learn to do this like you?" asked the student.

"By coming to know your true self," answered the grandmaster.

"When shall we start that lesson?" anxiously asked the student.

"Tomorrow," calmly said the grandmaster.

**BEFORE YOU,
THERE WAS CHUNG DOE,
THE PATHWAY THAT
HAS ITS SOURCE IN THE
ALL-POWERFUL UNIVERSAL GOD.**

初志一貫

Attain one's
(original)
object.

1

KNOW YOURSELF

CHUNG DOE AND PA DOE

THE FIRST STEP OF MOO DOE is to learn to know your true (pure) self in all aspects: mental, physical, spiritual, and in relationships with others. Those who achieve such self-knowledge are prepared to choose and follow the right path. There are two paths in life—Chung Doe (leading to success) and Pa Doe (leading to failure). Chung Doe is the way of great mental, physical, and spiritual power that adds value to the individual, family, and others. Relationships based on the principles of the Chung Doe pathway are pure, enduring, and productive of the "good seed" to leave behind for the family and coming generations. Pa Doe is the "bad seed" of Moo Doe morals, because it lives only unto itself without connection to eternal principles. You have the power to choose the path that you will take. How will you choose? By learning to know your (pure) self and by following these principles, you shall find the path.

- Life is a never-ending challenge for good and for bad. You have the power to choose the good path and become as great as you want.
- You are your own guide. You are your own guard.
- The "unseeing" can harm themselves. The "unknowing" can harm others. That is Pa Doe.
- Those that see and know are a light to themselves and a beacon to others. That is Chung Doe.
- You are your own mirror. You are your own light.
- Chung Doe brings you into deep, still water that moves with eternal purpose. Deep is strong. The deeper the water, the stronger the power.
- Stillness is the voice of destiny.
- Through Chung Doe, you can achieve peace and security.
- Choose your teachers carefully; as they are, you will become.
- Great strength of mind and body in harmony: that is the goal, that is the challenge of life.

The Dragonfly's Reflection

On a beautiful clear day, the grandmaster and his student were strolling beside a crystal pond. The scent of cherry blossoms filled the air. "See the dragonfly over there?" remarked the student. "It sits upon its own image on the water, next to the lotus flower."

"What question does it ask you?" questioned the grandmaster.

"What do you mean?" asked the student.

"It asks, 'How long have you known yourself?'" replied the grandmaster.

"How long have I known myself?" confusingly replied the student. "Well, my whole life! What sort of question is that?"

"How do you look?" asked the grandmaster.

"Just as I look in the water. See my image reflected there!" said the student.

"Close your eyes. Now, how do you look?" asked the grandmaster.

Somewhat reluctantly the student closed his eyes and answered, "I see some of my features, but dimly."

"With Moo Doe," said the grandmaster, "you will learn to see yourself clearly—not only the visible you, but the invisible you."

"How can I see the invisible me?" asked the student.

The grandmaster smiled, and then said: "The correct path begins when you humbly ask: 'Who am I?' The most important thing is to learn to know your true self, your pure self. That is the first step of Moo Doe. Most

23

people, when they close their eyes, see nothing. They are then gone, because their self-image is a fleeting shadow. They do not know themselves. Worse yet, they do not know that they do not know themselves."

"How can I know myself clearly?" asked the young student.

"It is both a choice and a way," replied the grandmaster.

"I am confused. What do you mean?" asked the student.

"It is a choice," explained the grandmaster, "because you have the power to become as great as you want. It is a way because you can move forward day-by-day along the correct path toward knowing your inner self."

"Who shall guide me?" asked the worried student.

"You shall guide yourself," said the grandmaster, "using correct principles. You are your own guide. You are your own guard, no matter where you are."

"My own guard?" asked the student with surprise.

"Moo Doe is the path leading to true mental, physical, and spiritual power," explained the grandmaster. "It is both dangerous and secure. For those who do not know themselves, it is a path of danger, because the 'unseeing' can harm themselves, and the 'unknowing' can damage others. That is Pa Doe. But for those who see and know, Moo Doe points to a way of security, for they are their own guards. They are a light to themselves and a beacon to others. They are on the Chung Doe pathway, and that is the pathway of wisdom."

"Am I on such a path?" ambitiously asked the student.

"Look at what you did today. What do you see?" questioned the grandmaster.

"I see myself strolling and learning," answered the student.

"When you learn to know your true self, your pure self," continued the grandmaster. "You will see yourself without using a mirror." The grandmaster stopped walking for a moment. He faced the student and placed his hands on the shoulders of the younger man and said, "Look at the spot of dirt on your face."

The student blinked his eyes in surprise and asked, "What dirt?"

With the back of his fingers, the grandmaster brushed away the spot of dirt from the student's cheek and told the student: "You could not see it nor feel it, but soon you will know with certainty when such an intrusion occurs, for you will see it and feel it with your inner self. You are your own guard. If you are deep and still, you can purify yourself, both visible and invisible."

"Deep and still?" asked the student.

"Like this deep pond," replied the grandmaster. "By contrast, shallow water can be noisy, with much splashing. Pa Doe is shallow and noisy. Chung Doe brings you into deep, still water that moves slowly with principle. Depth brings forth power. The deeper the water, the stronger the power. Stillness is the voice of destiny."

"How soon shall I find myself?" wondered the student.

The grandmaster reached down and gathered a handful of sand and said: "The steps you follow along the correct path are like these small grains of sand. When they are cemented together and formed into bricks, they become the building blocks of self-knowledge. I will teach you the principles, but you must act for yourself. I will bring you to the banquet of learning, but you must eat on your own, and at your own pace. That is the principle of learning."

"Is the way hard?" meekly asked the student.

"To construct the building of self-knowledge is hard," explained the grandmaster, "but the rewards are great. Once you have finished the task, you will feel secure within your building, your temple of wisdom. You will feel at peace no matter what storms may descend upon you. Then, no matter where you are, you will have harmony and inner peace, for the building of wisdom is within you. And with care, the building will last forever."

The student lowered his head in a serious attitude. Then, lifting his gaze to the grandmaster once again, he said. "How soon can I be like you? Is this even possible?"

The grandmaster smiled as he caught a glimpse of the dragonfly alighting on the surface of the water nearby. Concentric circles expanded in the sunlight and the grandmaster replied, "It is indeed possible. You are now ready. Tomorrow we begin."

THE LESSON

Throughout the history of Moo Doe in East Asia, the grandmasters have always taught about two paths that Moo Doe can follow. One is "Chung Doe," or the right path, and the other is "Pa Doe," or the wrong path. Chung Doe is one of the main principles of correct Moo Doe. Those who develop a deep sense of self-knowledge as they follow the Chung Doe pathway will more easily remain on course. Therefore, the first step of Moo Doe is to learn to know your true (pure) self.

Why is this so important? Those who follow Chung Doe value the principles of honor, integrity, loyalty, and compassion above all else, and live their lives accordingly.

Someone who follows the Chung Doe pathway of Moo Doe considers the consequences to others involved before making any decision fully. When Moo Doe follows the Chung Doe path, the focus is on building character, confidence, self-esteem, and strength. Those who choose to follow the principles of Chung Doe are extremely strong--even into their 70s and longer--and their techniques and movements are very powerful.

This same strength will carry over into their daily lives, which will be enriched, thus enabling them to find balance. Chung Doe uses the power of Moo Doe only for the right reason (correct justice) to purify family relations, friendships, spirituality, and daily activities. Chung Doe leaves the "good seed" behind within the family and others. The good seed of Moo Doe morals and wisdom leads to the good fruit of right communication, compassion, and integrity as a legacy for the next generation. Over the centuries, a tremendous number of humans have followed Chung Doe for success in their lives. This path earns the recognition and respect of others and leaves behind the memory of a good name--one sure way to attain a truly meaningful and successful life.

On the other hand, those who choose to follow Pa Doe (the wrong path) are known for their egotism, jealousy, and lack of sterling qualities such as honor, discipline, and stability. Their troublemaking and selfishness cause them to believe in a distortion of reality that is far from enduring truth. They do not know themselves and their own potential; worse still, they do not know that they do not know themselves (ignorance of the pure truth). Thus they act in a state of unknowing and disharmony. Their noisemaking and clamor cause them to be deaf to the promptings of destiny. Their self-love causes them to be blind to the light of goodness and service to others. They are drunk with their own small thoughts; they are carried down by their own petty self-interests. Pa Doe is the "bad seed" that leads to bitter fruit and dishonor.

The True (Pure) Self Is Unassailable

With the invisible eye, you view yourself perpetually in the image of your highest potential as In Gan--humanness at its root center. No matter what your circumstances, no matter what others might say of you, no matter how you might be judged or misjudged, you are that true self that you see with the invisible eye. You are the mountain, not a fleeting wisp of smoke; the rock, not a dry leaf spiraling down in the wind; the ocean, not a dying ember in the night. Mountain is mountain; rock is rock; ocean is ocean. You are your own true self forever, moving constantly upward along the Chung Doe pathway, toward a clear vision of In Gan. That is the principle of the true (pure) self. That is your choice.

Travelers along the Pa Doe pathway have also made a choice. They choose not to see themselves in the light of their own potential greatness. Instead, they choose to close their eyes and fall, to tumble down and around through corridors of chaos, leading nowhere. They are drunk on their own selfish ideas and blind to their own potential. They are ignorant of the principle that to lose yourself in service to others is to find yourself in a state of joy. Worse still, they are unaware that they are unaware. Thus, in their unknowing state, they are open to becoming a danger to themselves and others.

THE WEAPON THAT IS NO WEAPON

Because Pa Doe travelers choose to fall, they would have others fall too. To that end, they deploy their secret weapons of the night--whispered lies, greedy gossip, and character assassination. In their envy, jealousy, and insecurity, they seek to destroy the reputation of the Chung Doe traveler. They say, "The mountain is a charade. The rock is drifting sand. The ocean is mere vapor." To the uncertain, this weapon is terrifying. But to the self-knowing human this weapon is no weapon at all, because the self-knowing human being is anchored in the vision of who that human being is: he or she knows who he or she is. Thus, the self-knowing human is unassailable.

THREE SHIELDS AGAINST SLANDER

Throughout history, human beings of strong character have learned how to stand firm in the face of malicious rumor-mongering. In the system of Moo Doe morals, the Chung Doe traveler deflects the assault of slander in three key ways:

Vision - Stay focused on the true (pure) self, cleansed of the negative. Keep the invisible eye open to the vision of the pure self, uneclipsed by the fogs of calumny and the mists of reproach.

Light - Gather the facts. When the winds of rumor blow, practice and teach others the principle of not drawing any conclusions in the absence of observable, confirmed facts. Bring light into the situation before making any judgments or acting on information supplied by others.

Action - Keep moving forward and upward on the Chung Doe pathway, no matter what. Refuse to be distracted. Life is a never-ending challenge for good and for bad. This you cannot change. But you can continually choose the good way and cultivate the good seeds to leave behind for your family.

There is honor that needs to be preserved, marriages that need to be purified so that no negative elements can come in, children who need to be shown how to live by principle, and communities that need to be given better leadership of enlightenment. All of this depends on knowing the true self. In the true (pure) self there is great power to ward off the hurtful forces swirling all around us to dim the light of self-knowledge and declare principle void. But these forces wither in the face of Moo Doe power like blades of dry grass in a fiery furnace.

HOW TO CULTIVATE A PURE RELATIONSHIP

Learning to know your true (pure) self means knowing yourself physically, mentally, spiritually, and in relationships with others. To gain extraordinary strength and vitality, the Chung Doe traveler trains and disciplines his or her mind, body, and spirit to draw from the limitless reserve of energy in the universe. He or she aligns action with natural and eternal principle. Negative influences are purged before they can have a destructive effect.

The same applies to the Chung Doe way of building relationships. Such relationships endure because they are rooted in the principle of continual service and the mutual goal of cultivating a lasting legacy for the family and the coming generations. Purity of relationship is essential to this mission. Just as we guard against exposing the body to germs, we also guard against allowing damaging influences to enter into the relationship. If there is even a tiny crack in the relationship, toxic elements can enter. The relationship remains open to new ideas, creative solutions, loving suggestions, and the corrective example of Moo Doe role models. But the relationship remains closed to antagonism, envy, and any influence that generates dishonor, lack of togetherness, or the destruction of the good name of the family. Therefore, how urgent it is to purify the relationship, to make it secure and immune to Pa Doe effects. Pure friendship and pure love characterize the relationship between and among Chung Doe travelers.

THE ANATOMY OF A RELATIONSHIP

In marriage, in friendships, and in business, relationships often erode because the parties become misaligned and the harmony fades. Those who endeavor to strengthen and firm up a relationship through will power and heroic effort often fail. A metal rod bent and straightened repeatedly over and over again at the same spot will heat up, become brittle, and snap. The same thing can happen in a relationship. There is much call, in recent times, to take action to strengthen marriages and families. The cause is urgent, but are the voices calling for the correct strategies? Is it enough to tighten down with greater force? Is it enough for the parties to focus on pleasing each other at all costs? Is there relief in seeking after perpetual variety, or in trying to remember every favorite aspect of someone's life, or in living primarily in the past, or in the present, or in the future?

If the relationship is based on such patterns, then danger looms, for sooner or later someone will forget something, and the other party will be hurt. When the pressure builds up over time, the relationship develops cracks, and negative elements creep in to destroy it. Eventually, this situation leaves us feeling alone. When that happens, the desire swells to empty the cup and fill it with a new relationship, or to abandon the old cup and start with another.

How urgent it is, therefore, for each human being to learn his or her true (pure) self and cultivate pure relationships that reflect the values of harmony, balance, integrity, loyalty, and commitment to the mutual vision of service and to leave behind a good name for the family. Enduring relationships are sustained by wisdom. Pure love is not carefree nor closed. The parties in such relationship are not too close and not too far away from each other. They stand in just the correct proximity. If the situation is severely tightened down, it can become brittle and break. If it is maintained too loosely, or disconnected, other influences can wedge themselves in between and start their work of destruction. But if the relationship is supple, agile, and responsibly close, then both parties apply the true (pure) self to the mutual objective of obtaining harmony, balance, joy, and peace; thus, transforming the bond into one that endures forever.

A RELATIONSHIP BUILT ON A ROCK

A promise written in sand, or nest built in tumbleweed, a pillow made of chaff--all these are more enduring than a relationship built on momentary truth. In all relationships, the time comes when the parties open up to each other to bare their innermost thoughts and feelings. This is the "truth of the moment." The parties say to themselves, "We have revealed our deepest soul to each other. Now we have lasting trust between us, because we know things about each other that no one else knows."

But such truth is not a solid foundation for a relationship. Such truth can change because it comes from thoughts. Thoughts come from the mind, and does the mind not change things? How can a relationship be safely moored to a drifting dock? How can loyalty to a phantom truth be defended? When that truth changes in a human being, another is often unaware of the transition to a new momentary truth. Discovering it after the fact is often a shock: the result can be hurt and anger. Thus the relationship erodes and those who were once close are now distant and troubled. It need not be that way. A relationship built on principle endures because principle never changes. Principle is eternal truth, a solid mooring for a relationship. These are eight mooring lines for your enduring relationships.

1. **Know your true (pure) self.** If you learn to see yourself with the invisible eye, if you have come to know your true (pure) self, you are filled with confident hope for the future and certainty about success. You know your identity: You are not smoke, or a dry leaf, or a dying ember, but mountain, rock, ocean. And this certainty imparts strength to your relationships, your spouse, and your children. It makes your bonds last forever.

2. **Choose the "Correct" (The Moo Doe Moral Compass).** If you learn to make correct choices based on unchanging principle, choosing to do that which will do the most good for each member of the family and other loved ones, you will never suffer the pain of a fading relationship based on the shifting truth of the moment. The parties to the relationship are not defensive, since there is no contest to see who is "right" or who is the "winner," and there is no need for a human being to put another on the defensive over trivial matters or misunderstandings. Simply refocus and move on.

3. **Overcome Doe Chi.** If you stay connected to the enduring root, rather than to the shifting branches and falling leaves, the relationship will receive constant nourishment and will be immune to the weakening pressures of blaming others, retreating into failure, or allowing self-pride to turn back genuine counsel and suggestions--all Doe Chi tactics.

4. **Leave behind the good seeds.** If you stay committed to cultivating the invisible fruits of character, balance, peace, and strength with family and others, you need never become obsessed with the visible, tangible things that fade with time and are soon forgotten after you die. You own and enjoy visible things, but they do not own you.

5. **Seek the face of honor.** If you constantly seek to cultivate honor in your relationships, you can dispose of the artificial masks of Keum Soo--

humanness in its wild animal (out of control beast) aspect: greed, selfishness, envy, and alienation. These are the masks that destroy togetherness and undermine love and loyalty.

6. **Change your reality.** If you learn to change your reality on a daily basis in meaningful ways, you can protect the relationship from stagnation, deadened lassitude, and hurt feelings.

7. **Become a living vessel of wisdom.** If you learn to become the source of wisdom, then your relationship develops the rhythms of success, and you climb from one mountain to the next, rather than lapsing into the downward spiral of Gan Sa—the addiction to shifting appetite and endless variety.

8. **Draw on nature's power through Nae Gong.** If you learn and practice the exquisite exercises and movements of Nae Gong, you will draw extraordinary strength from the unlimited source of energy in the universe and, thus, infuse enduring resiliency and vitality into your relationships.

You can achieve all these benefits through *The Master Key of Wisdom*. These are the lifelong fruits of harmony, peace, joy, service, honor, togetherness, faith, and great internal and external strengths. These are the benefits that flow to the Chung Doe travelers. The system of Moo Doe morals forms the foundation for spiritual growth-- how to "win yourself" so that you know how to control yourself in any circumstance and prepare the way for a place in the heavenly realms. Relationships based on such principles last forever. Thus, you maintain that beautiful harmonious balance--not too close, not too far away--that is characteristic of an enduring partnership. The choice is yours.

The Voice as the Signature of the Self

Pure relationships are cultivated with a discerning ear. The true (pure) self listens to the voices of fellow travelers and chooses friendships correctly and wisely. Every human being has three main kinds of voices to listen to:

1. **The Voice of Chung Doe** - Words, tones, and volume that tend to cultivate harmony, balance, togetherness, respect, honor, and dignity. The strategy is service and cultivating the good seed. The discourse is straight, direct, dignified, and self-effacing. For example, similar to the deep, still water in the ocean that moves inexorably forward with power and purpose.

2. **The Voice of Emptiness** - Words, tones, and volume designed only to fill the silence with idle talk and aimless superficialities, or to draw attention to the speaker. The strategy is to spend time. The discourse is rambling, circular, and shallow. For example, similar to the eddies going nowhere at the edge of a stream.

3. **The Voice of Pa Doe** - Words, tones, and volume designed to secure specific personal benefit or advantage to the speaker. The nature of such a voice is self-serving. The strategy is manipulation. The tone is shrill, boastful, and arrogant (Doe Chi). The volume is loud and boisterous. For example, similar to the seething, muddy torrent of wash in the gutter after a sudden storm: quick, gaudy, and full of garbage.

The Chung Doe traveler discerns the voices and forms alliances only with those who speak the Moo Doe language of destiny.

CONCLUSION

Learning to know the true (pure) self is the beginning of your journey along the upward rising Chung Doe pathway. The journey is not without its challenges, for life is a never-ending challenge for good or for bad. By choosing the good way, you will come to know your great mental, physical, and spiritual capacity, and grow to see the achievement of this limitless potential. By using Moo Doe morals, you will build pure relationships that will help you cultivate the good seeds to leave for your family and others: harmony, peace, joy, service, honor, faith, and lasting love of togetherness. Authentic, traditional Moo Doe, as passed down over the centuries, is directly concerned with helping seekers achieve balance of mind, body, and spirit. Insincere and pretentious Pa Doe influence can produce no such good effects. Remember, you can borrow knowledge from another, but you cannot borrow a body, a mind, or a spirit. These are yours alone to develop through great discipline, resolve, and effort. You can pretend to have balance, vitality, and strength, but these qualities in their genuine form can be achieved only after much effort based on correct principles and knowledge of the true (pure) self. Over the centuries millions have found the answer through Moo Doe wisdom, following the Chung Doe pathway.

**GREAT STRENGTH
OF MIND AND BODY
IN HARMONY:
THAT IS THE GOAL
OF SELF-KNOWLEDGE**

苦盡甘來

pain is gone,
pleasure is come.

2

CHOOSE THE CORRECT

THE MOO DOE MORAL COMPASS

THE SECOND STEP OF MOO DOE is to learn how to choose the Correct each day. By knowing your true self, you will know your true feelings—what is True for you in a given situation. By following the Chung Doe pathways of honor and integrity, you will also know what is Right and what is "not right" for the individual, for the family, and for others. By seeking to balance the True and the Right, you will see more clearly the Correct choices for daily action leading to greater peace and joy. That is Moo Doe power and harmony.

- The True, the Right, and the Correct are your companions for life. How you deal with them each day will determine how much peace you will enjoy.
- The way of Moo Doe is to balance the True with the Right and arrive at the Correct. You do this by using the Moo Doe moral compass.
- Balance is reached through the gateway of Correct living. Joy and peace are the fruits of balance. This is the challenge of life, the way of success.
- Pa Doe sees from only one side; Chung Doe sees from all sides. Pa Doe is for the good of one; Chung Doe is for the good of many. Pa Doe follows its own selfish voice; Chung Doe follows the voice of the Correct. Pa Doe leads to pain and isolation; Chung Doe leads to balance and peace.
- With the outcome of Chung Doe, all things (balance, harmony, power, and peace) are possible.

Great strength of mind and body in harmony: that is where the Moo Doe moral compass leads you.

The Fruits of Balance

After nature had poured a gentle rain over the earth, the dawn brought warmth to the countryside. Footsteps announced a visitor to the cottage of the grandmaster. It was his student who gingerly knocked on the door and softly asked, "Grandmaster, are you awake?"

"Over here," called out a voice from behind an apple tree in a nearby orchard. Startled, the student turned and peered directly into the rising sun in the direction of the voice and asked, "Is that you, Grandmaster?"

"Yes," replied the grandmaster.

"I am sorry to be a little late," responded the student, "but the pillow held me prisoner."

"You wanted to stay in bed this morning?" asked the grandmaster.

"No! That is, I..." stammered the student.

"Speak the truth!" demanded the grandmaster.

"Well, it was inviting," admitted the student.

"Why did you not follow your true feelings and stay in bed?" questioned the grandmaster.

"Because of my appointment to see you and receive a lesson," answered the student, "it was right to come."

"Your lesson has already started," replied the grandmaster. "You did the right thing to come. Those three fellows (the True, the Right, and the Correct) are your companions for life. Go to the deepest valley, and they are there. Go to the highest mountain, and they are there. Cross the widest sea, and they are already waiting for you. How you deal with these three companions will determine your course in life and how much peace you will enjoy."

"Can you explain further, Grandmaster?" asked the student.

The grandmaster smiled and said, "Here, let us pick one of these apples. Do they not look delicious? Go ahead. Pick one."

"How do you feel about the apple?" questioned the grandmaster.

"Well, it looks good, and I came away in a hurry without any breakfast," answered the student with hunger.

"So you truly want one?" teased the grandmaster.

"Well, yes, it is the truth, but...," stuttered the student.

"What if I told you that the farmer gave me permission to take fruit from this tree?" asked the grandmaster, as he reached up and picked one of the most beautiful apples.

"Then it would be the correct thing to do?" wondered the student.

The grandmaster handed him the apple and said, "Already you are beginning to understand. Hold the apple until we get to the village. I have someone I want you to meet."

As the two made their way down the puddle roadway, a woman on a loaded bicycle hurried past them. Suddenly the bicycle tire hit a hole full of rainwater and sent a spray of mud over the student.

"See here! Look what you have done to me!" angrily shouted the student.

Embarrassed, the woman stopped and returned to her victim. "I am sorry," she said, "but I will be late opening up my stall at the market."

"What do you sell?" asked the grandmaster.

"I weave baskets at night and sell them during the day to feed my family," she replied.

"At what time do you have to get up each morning?" questioned the grandmaster.

"At four o'clock," answered the woman.

"Do you like to get up so early?" he asked.

"No," she replied, "but I must work to care for my family. That is the right thing for me to do."

"Is it right for you to leave your children all day?" teased the grandmaster.

"Truly I would prefer to care for them myself," replied the woman, "and it is not right to leave them. But I must work to give them food."

"You act correctly," assured the grandmaster. "Your children will benefit from this correct judgment. And for this you will have peace. I am sure you have left your children in good hands. Have a pleasant day."

After the woman had pedaled away, the grandmaster asked his student, "Do you always conduct your life according to that which is true?"

"Of course," replied the student, somewhat offended at the question.

"How did you feel when the woman splashed you with mud?" asked the grandmaster.

"Truly I felt like pushing her off the roadway and into the ditch," replied the student with great emotion.

"That was your true feeling?" asked the grandmaster.

"Yes," replied the student.

"Then, if you always act according to that which is true, why did you not do it?" questioned the grandmaster.

"Well, I guess," mumbled the student, "I guess that I decided that it would not be the right thing to do."

"By controlling your actions in this way," explained the grandmaster, "you did that which was correct. You are a good host to your three companions--the True, the Right, and the Correct. The way of the Chung Doe path is to balance the True with the Right and arrive at Correct."

By now, the grandmaster and his student had reached the village. The marketplace was buzzing with noise and activity.

"Follow me," said the grandmaster. The two made their way down a dark alley to a dingy shack in a deserted corner of the village.

"Look through this window and tell me what you see," instructed the grandmaster.

The student shielded his eyes from the morning sun and peered into the darkness. He saw there before him an old man in rags cowering in the corner.

"A beggar," said the student. "How does he endure the cold and the unhealthy conditions of this lonely place?"

"Hello, my friend. How do you feel today?" asked the grandmaster to the stranger.

"I endure. Thank you for coming again," whispered the old man.

After turning to the student, the grandmaster inquired, "How do you feel about this old man suffering alone here?"

"I would truly like to rescue him from this state," replied the student.

"Then why don't you do it? Truly you can find a way to change things for him," suggested the grandmaster.

"I see that it would not be right," said the student, "for how can I rescue him if he will not rescue himself?"

"Then you will do nothing?" asked the grandmaster.

The student hesitated for a minute, not knowing what to do. Then suddenly, he smiled broadly and said, "I will give him this apple. It is a start."

"That is correct," supportively said the grandmaster. "Though you would truly like to rescue him, it is not in your hands to do so. If he will not redirect his life on his own, you cannot force him. Thus, it is correct not to do so. The beggar has not followed the Chung Doe path. And though you truly would like to eat the apple yourself--and it would normally be right to do so--in this case, it is more right to care for the beggar. You may do the correct thing now."

Beaming with joy, the student reached through the window and handed the apple to the grateful beggar.

"Bless you, young man," said the old man, "and bless your master, for he has taught you kindness in your youth."

As the grandmaster and his student returned to the countryside, they felt the healing rays of the sun warming their bodies.

"How do you feel?" asked the grandmaster.

"I have joy and I have peace," replied the student.

"Joy and peace are the fruits of balance," stated the grandmaster. "And balance is reached through the gateway of correct living. Just as the sun frees you from the shadow of night, choosing the correct way will free you from the shadow of selfishness, imbalance, and lack of honor. That is Moo Doe harmony. That is Moo Doe power, the path to a successful life. Now, let us go and pick more apples."

"How can I learn more, Grandmaster?" intriguingly asked the student.

"In the next lesson," calmly replied the grandmaster.

THE LESSON

Throughout history, those who have practiced Moo Doe morals by following the Chung Doe pathway have used a powerful system for making Correct decisions. This system is based on a triangle of relationships.

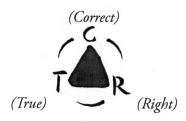

(Correct)

(True)   *(Right)*

The True refers to your inner state at any given time--how you truly feel about something. This inner state might be joy, anger, fear, sadness, or love. How you feel about something (the True) largely determines what you choose to do about it. Thus, the True leads to choice that leads to one or more possible actions in response to the circumstances.

The True ⟶ Choice ⟶ Action

But which, if any, of these possible actions is the Right thing to do under the circumstances? By the Right we mean doing the most good for everyone involved, causing the most long-term growth, harmony, joy, peace, and well-being.

The choice of action that will do the most good for everyone involved is called the Correct choice (balance

49

and harmony). The goal is to do that which is Correct in all aspects of daily living: personal, marriage and family relationships, professional, community, and spiritual.

To use a simple illustration: Suppose a parent notices one of his or her children having difficulty solving a homework problem. The parent feels deep compassion for the child. Thus, in this case, the True is compassion. What should be done? The parent has many choices, which include:

1. Scold the child for lack of self-reliance;
2. Do the problem for the child;
3. Instruct the child to ask the teacher for help the next day; or
4. Teach the child the principles behind the problem and let the child follow through on his own.

The parent wishes to cultivate self-respect and independent thinking in the child; therefore, the parent chooses action #4, which turns out to be the Correct choice in this case. There may be circumstances where the other choices would be Correct, but not in this example.

Thus, when the True is balanced with the Right, the choice leads to the Correct. In this sense, the triangle system serves as a compass to guide you to Correct behavior in daily life based on principles of Moo Doe morals.

THE MOO DOE MORAL COMPASS

(Correct)

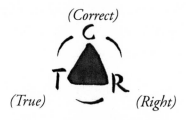

(True)   *(Right)*

HOW TO USE THE MOO DOE COMPASS

The Moo Doe moral compass has been handed down over the centuries to help practitioners of Moo Doe morals make the correct decisions for daily living. This compass is not held in the hand, but is located within every living human being. It is based on correct thinking and correct judgment. Therefore, it is often likened to the "conscience." To know the true self is to become fully aware of this special compass and how to use it to increase the well-being of the individual, the family, and others, and to achieve great internal and external strength, peace, and freedom.

The climb to the summit of Moo Doe power and harmony is beset with many challenges and obstacles. The Chung Doe pathway--based on honor, integrity, discipline, loyalty, and service to others--leads to the top. The Moo Doe moral compass assures success in this quest. By using your conscience (head) to balance the True and the Right, you can achieve the Correct in daily living and mark the milestones of achievement on this journey.

On the other hand, the Pa Doe pathway (the wrong path)--based on selfishness, greed, empty boastfulness, and careless use of power--leads to dark by-ways and dead-end detours. The Pa Doe follower fails to follow his moral compass for staying on course and, therefore, all too quickly wanders from the way of victory and falls short of the mark. Based on what he believes, the Pa Doe follower makes decisions based only on the True or only on the Right, without thought of the Correct.

THE MORAL COMPASS LEADS TO POWER AND FREEDOM

By applying the Chung Doe pathway--with a balancing of the True and the Right to reach the Correct--you will have power. This true power is the product of five positive abilities, which are:

1. Understanding better;

2. Acquiring more knowledge;

3. Gaining better positions;

4. Making the correct choices; and,

5. Exercising good judgment through wisdom.

Through this power you will have true freedom, living for tomorrow. What happens when you fail to use the moral compass? When you fail to make decisions based on the triangle of True/Right/Correct, you have no power. Arrogant humans are only fooling themselves, believing that they have power when they do not. Arrogance deceives human beings into believing that they have freedom. What kind of freedom is there in being alone? Alone helps no one. Where are your "earnings" (your value) if you are alone? They are nonexistent.

Arrogance is the Pa Doe pathway (the wrong way). The Pa Doe follower is an individual on an island. He is king. He owns everything on his island. What does this mean? Because he is alone, it means nothing. When you are alone, you talk only to the wind.

The Pa Doe follower hears only what he wants to hear out of all that is being said. He then uses his "selective hearing" to his advantage. He also releases his own pain by thriving on the pain of others. He relishes gossip. He thrives on backbiting. He pretends to help others and please them, when in truth he is deceiving them while trying to increase his own worth. He does not follow the Moo Doe moral compass but responds instead to a compass of ego and self-promotion. He aspires to the top but uses a strategy that will consign him to the bottom. Truly Pa Doe actions are influenced from the "dark (evil) side."

BEWARE OF DOE CHI

How is it that some humans follow the Pa Doe pathway (the wrong pathway)? How is it they fail to follow their internal moral compass? The answer is Doe Chi--being drunk on one's (your) own thoughts and words. Doe Chi is a form of tunnel vision where only self-interest is visible, where the viewer can only see a narrow space directly in front, but never the whole picture. How can you arrive at correct decisions for the good of everyone involved when you see only yourself, alone within your confined space?

Consider a vase. How do you judge its condition? If you look at the vase from one side only and see no cracks, you could conclude that the vase is whole. But what if there are cracks on the hidden side? If you do not see the complete picture, you cannot arrive at correct decisions. Beware! This is Doe Chi.

THE INNER WORKINGS OF THE MOO DOE MORAL COMPASS

The Moo Doe moral compass is an extraordinary tool. If you look at it with the invisible eye, you gain clarity about how it operates to help you make correct decisions that are based on, but transcend, decisions based on just the True or the Right. The True is connected to that part of you that gathers sensations through the senses (sight, hearing, touch, taste, smell). These sensations combine to give you a first wave of perception, which registers upon your mind and contributes to how you "feel" about your experience in a given moment. What you feel in a given moment is what is True for you--the "truth of the moment."

For example, suppose you are walking down the street and see a man bolt suddenly from a store and knock another man to the ground. Your first impression is that this behavior is violent and cruel. Your "momentary truth" is that the man from the store is the aggressor and needs to be stopped. You are strongly motivated to rescue the man on the ground by using force. Based on your current level of understanding, this action would be Right.

But wait. A woman then runs out of the store and points to the man, who is now struggling to wrest himself free from his captor. "He stole my purse," she screams. At that point, you notice the man on the ground is clutching a woman's purse within the folds of his jacket. This throws new light on the situation and you immediately step in and help restrain the culprit.

By gaining more perspective on the situation, you are able to observe things in a wider context and in greater detail. Your mind has extended its span of understanding significantly, so that you are now seeing more clearly what was earlier too distant for you. At the same time, you are now seeing from far away (i.e., from the perspective of unchanging principle) what was earlier too close to you (your "momentary truth"). Thus you are now more likely to choose the correct course of action.

By using the Moo Doe moral compass, you are able to see distant things up close, and close things at a distance. You begin to rise to the level of wisdom, where your actions will begin to produce the good seeds of balance, harmony, peace, and joy.

Three Levels of Light

You can see that the Moo Doe moral compass operates on the basis of three kinds of light.

Level One: Dim Light
(perception of the senses)

We have the impression that this level of light is very bright and clear. We see things in all of their colors; we hear sounds clearly, and so on. However, this is a delusion. Such light is very dim. It illuminates only enough to give us momentary truth, and momentary truth can change very quickly. Many actions down through the centuries have been based on momentary truth, which often leads to misunderstanding, strained relationships, disagreement, and anger. What has seemed right at the moment has not produced more harmony, but more misunderstanding and more disagreement.

Level Two: Moderate Light
(understanding of the mind)

By expanding our perspective and integrating what we perceive into the larger body of our experience over time, we bring still more light into the situation. Our actions, therefore, are more likely to be correct. Even this is not sufficient, because our Right decisions are based on only our perceptions and understanding that may not produce the most good for the most humans, and therefore are not correct. What is missing is the enduring connection to unchanging principle, which is discovered in the next level.

LEVEL THREE: BRIGHT LIGHT
(WISDOM OF THE INVISIBLE EYE)

When we open the invisible (spiritual) eye and view the situation from the perspective of unchanging principle, we make our decisions based on wisdom. Such decisions are always correct, because wisdom guides us to act in the interests of producing more harmony, peace, joy, vitality, and lasting strength for everyone involved.

Therefore, in using the Moo Doe moral compass of True/Right/Correct, remember that it guides you to higher and higher levels of light and wisdom. As you progress along the Chung Doe pathway and gain more experience and wisdom, you will come to make correct decisions quite naturally using this higher form of light. It is very much like passing by someone who is eating a delicious red apple and your mouth waters. Your sensation comes from your experience of eating apples. Hence, when you come to use wisdom naturally, you will know very quickly what is correct in life. That is the operation of the higher light. That is the principle of growth and success. To achieve this success is the highest challenge of life, leading to the greatest benefits that endure forever.

CONCLUSION

Whatever you want in life, no matter what you are, you can reach it and surpass it by using the Moo Doe moral compass of True/Right/Correct to guide your decisions. You must use this compass in governing all areas of your life, especially to be correct in your treatment of marriage, children, parents, friendship, health, employment, personal actions, and humanity--even something as simple as taking the time for food preparation. In all of these areas you can act with conviction by following your internal moral compass. Learn from your conscience, not from your mistakes. The compass is effective and sure; learning by mistakes is wasteful and uncertain. Getting sidetracked through needless mistakes wastes time--time that is never recovered. For example, if you travel a day off course, you lose two--the day it takes to return, plus the day it takes to catch up. Excuses are worthless and destructive as well as incorrect. Thus, balance True with Right to arrive with certainty at Correct.

As you travel through life, your legacy is greater through your "earnings" (doing good). By following the Chung Doe pathway to your ultimate summit, you will consistently use your inner moral compass as a guide. Using your head in this way, with good judgment and correct decision-making, you will increase in power and freedom. Through this freedom, you can accomplish balance and harmony. From this you can gain peace.

With the outcomes of Chung Doe--balance, harmony, power, and peace--all things are possible. Unless you stay firmly in charge of your forward progress by following your moral compass, there is no guidance. Without using your head in this way, how can you feel your heart? With no heart there is no hope. With no hope, there is no life. There is nothing.

How important is the Moo Doe moral compass? When following the Chung Doe path, you see that your compass is worth everything--even life itself. The decision is yours. Your choices and actions will be your future.

**GREAT STRENGTH OF
MIND AND BODY IN HARMONY
THAT IS WHERE THE
MOO DOE COMPASS
LEADS YOU**

心身鍛錬

Discipline
your mind
and body.

3

OVERCOME DOE CHI

THE THIRD STEP OF MOO DOE is to open the gate to your truly highest potential (e.g., In Gan) by overcoming "Doe Chi." Doe Chi means being drunk with one's (your) own thoughts and ideas. Doe Chi is blind to the needs and interests of others. By being stuck on True or Right, Doe Chi never arrives at Correct. Doe Chi is the master of fleeting illusions and selfish interests. The Doe Chi traveler follows the Pa Doe pathway of noise and whim. The In Gan traveler follows the Chung Doe pathway of stillness and power. The Doe Chi traveler goes alone. The In Gan traveler goes with genuine friends. These are the principles of overcoming Doe Chi.

- Doe Chi is the grand enemy of principle, the adversary of the Correct.
- Just as a dust storm obscures the vision of the sun, Doe Chi obscures the vision of Correct.
- You can borrow knowledge from others, but not wisdom. Wisdom must be earned.
- In the root is visible/invisible power, for the root endures. In Gan is humanness at its root center. The In Gan path is the way to success.
- Likes and dislikes change with the moment. Principles never change.
- A genuine friend tempers your mind again and again until it becomes a sword of power.
- You can change your reality. That is why life is full of hope, excitement, and challenge.
- Throughout history, those living within Doe Chi are not only alone and lonely, but are also failures at and within life.
- Life is a challenge for power. Power is strength. Without strength, you will not have power. Without power, you will never find freedom. With freedom, there is peace.

The Learning Tree

The grandmaster and his student made their way slowly up a hillside on a windy spring afternoon.

"It takes much power to climb uphill against the wind," noted the student.

"It does indeed," agreed the grandmaster. "Life is a challenge for power. Through power, you will find freedom. If there is no power, there is no hope and no freedom. With freedom, there is peace."

"What do you mean?" asked the student.

"See that great tree over there? What do you hear?" replied the grandmaster.

"I hear the wind rustling in the leaves and I hear the brushing together of the branches and the creaking of the trunk," answered the student.

"Do you hear the root?" asked the grandmaster.

"No," replied the student, "of course not."

"The root is growling like a tiger," said the grandmaster.

"Growling like a tiger? I hear nothing," said the student.

"Listen," whispered the grandmaster, "the root roars out a Moo Doe lesson. If you have ears, you can hear that which is still. If you have eyes, you can see that which is invisible."

"Help me understand, Grandmaster," pleadingly replied the student.

"The rustling leaves and flowers are but temporary," explained the grandmaster. "They do their part, then they are gone—the mere shadow of life. The branches sway and weave in the wind, bending with every gust. The trunk hardly moves, because it is stronger against outside pressures. But the real strength is in the root. The root feels nothing from the outside. This is the visible, invisible power."

"Visible, invisible?" asked the student.

"Visible to the outer eye through the growth of the tree," replied the grandmaster. "And the invisible power of the root you can see with our invisible eye and feel with your heart. Without this visible, invisible power of the root, the tree will die."

"And without the branches and leaves, the tree will also die," said the student.

The grandmaster smiled and said, "Seasons come and seasons go. From time to time the gardener wisely prunes back the branches. The autumn winds carry away the leaves. But the root endures."

"I see what you mean, Grandmaster," noted the student, "but my eyes are beguiled by the visible movement of the beautiful blossoms and leaves."

"They too speak a lesson," said the grandmaster. "Too easily they forget their invisible connections to the root. They swirl and twirl every which way the wind dictates. They hustle and bustle freely in the air. They speak with the voice of Doe Chi. They travel on the Pa Doe pathway. Their beauty is short-lived. The enduring beauty is in the root, because the root has visible/invisible power. The root speaks with the voice of In Gan--humanness at its root center. Such is the voice you hear on the Chung Doe pathway of principle and wisdom. Look again at the tree. What do you see now?"

"I see now the branches and the trunk of the tree," answered the student.

"The limbs sway and return to their place," continued the grandmaster. "When they sway, they depart again and again from the true straight path. But the trunk is more powerful. It moves ever so slightly when the wind becomes very strong."

"And the root," exclaimed the student, "is the most powerful of all!"

"Yes," replied the grandmaster. "Already you are seeing the visible, invisible power of Moo Doe. Follow the Chung Doe pathway from blossom to leaf to limb to trunk, and it leads you to the root, the source of the life of the tree. That is Moo Doe power (the road) related to daily activity. Where did this root come from to have so much power?"

"From a seed?" hesitantly answered the student.

"Yes," agreed the grandmaster. "From a mere seed that was part of a leaf cluster. Seed to root to seed again. That is the circle of living. In fact, it is like three circles: You are born with nothing. Everything you own during your lifetime is only temporary. And you take nothing with you when you die except your spirit. You leave behind a good role model--good seed."

By this time, the two had reached the top of the hill and were looking back down into the valley.

"What have you learned today?" asked the grandmaster.

"I have learned that the root strength is the visible, invisible power of Moo Doe," replied the student.

"Yes," said the grandmaster. "And if you follow the Chung Doe pathway, you will always come back to the source, to the root. That is the basis of your own power, your own root. You are 'In Gan.' You are solid. You are steady. You are powerful in your potential! Without this power, there is no living. And without living there is no power and no hope. For in living, you practice Moo Doe principles to strengthen the root. When you are strong in your center, you live the correct way. And when you live the correct way, you become strong in your center. That is balance. That is harmony, which leads to success in life. How do you feel?"

"I feel peaceful with this knowledge," answered the student.

"Good," replied the grandmaster, "it is the way of peace. Now let us return to the valley. We have much good to do before the sun will set."

"When can I learn more, Grandmaster?" eagerly asked the student.

"In the next lesson," calmly replied the grandmaster.

THE LESSON

You can borrow knowledge from another, but not wisdom. Wisdom must be earned. Over the centuries, the principles of Moo Doe have been passed down to help humans learn wisdom as they follow the Chung Doe pathway toward power, peace, and happiness.

At the end of the pathway is In Gan—the fulfillment of genuine humanness at its root center. As you are guided to make Correct decisions by balancing the True and the Right, you grow in strength and harmony and approach the ideal you were destined to become.

On the other hand, many humans transform themselves into something else. They become "Keum Soo," having the form of humanness, but acting more like out of control animals. This is superficial humanness--humanness only on the surface--seeking selfish choices for personal gains. At its heart, Keum Soo cultivates Doe Chi--the character of a person who is drunk on his or her own thoughts and ideas, believing what he or she wants to believe without fully understanding circumstances nor the consequences. Doe Chi is blind to the Correct, and thrives instead on the fleeting moment. Doe Chi is the master of selfishness, knowingly or unknowingly. Doe Chi cares nothing for the good of everyone involved, but only for oneself. Doe Chi follows the lonely Pa Doe pathway to Keum Soo. The road to nothingness.

SIX VOICES OF DOE CHI

Look at society today. On all sides there is evidence of Doe Chi. Typically, humans do not follow principles, but rather their momentary likes and dislikes. Likes and dislikes change constantly. Principles never change.

Doe Chi is the grand enemy of principles, the adversary of the Correct. Just as a dust storm obscures the vision of the sun, Doe Chi obscures the vision of the Correct. Many humans are stuck in today; when tomorrow comes, they are lost because they are not established on principles. They do not tap into the visible, invisible power of the root. They sway to and from with every gust of wind. They have prepared nothing. They have no power or peace. Doe Chi has many voices, and these are six of the most common heard today.

1. STUCK ON "TRUE"

You go to dinner with friends. You order lobster. One friend orders a fish entree. Another orders steak. "Why did you not order lobster?" you ask your friends. "Lobster is the best choice." They may answer you with: "Why did you not order fish (or steak)?" Everyone knows what he or she prefers. Everyone discovers the True. But very few understand that another's True may be different from their own. Quite often an individual compels others to accept his or her version of the True. He or she says, "You must see it my way." But what if his or her way is not in the best interest of everyone involved? Seeing it his or her way may seem right to that individual—out of self-interest—but it may not be Correct. "You must see it my way" is the voice of Doe Chi, and Doe Chi is the enemy of the Correct. "You must see it my way" has caused an endless array of violence and war throughout history. Look around you: everyone discovers the True, but very few discover the Correct.

2. Stuck on "Right"

Many insist that their way of doing things is the Right way, even though it may not serve the greater good of everyone involved. Have you seen adults who drive themselves relentlessly toward a goal, to the neglect of their families? They say, "I must reach my goal. I am doing it for them--my family." In reality they may be shortening their lives and denying their family a lasting legacy. "I must prove myself at all cost"—that is the voice of Doe Chi. Doe Chi gambles with the opportunities that rightfully belong to those who would otherwise benefit if that individual were following the Chung Doe pathway. Doe Chi is stubborn and selfish. Doe Chi wears the boastful face of Keum Soo.

3. Stuck on Not Knowing

What if we do not understand the principle of True/Right/Correct (the Moo Doe moral compass) and don't want to understand? Worse still: What if we don't even know we don't know? What if we are stuck in the passive mode of ignorance and just accept someone else's opinion of what is True and Right --and thus never arrive at Correct on our own? What if we bend like the limbs and leaves of the tree with every gust of wind? We are stuck at nowhere. We say, "They told me what to do." Our voice is the voice of Doe Chi. Doe Chi is lazy and listless when it comes to principle and genuine power. Doe Chi breeds weakness.

4. STUCK ON BLAMING OTHERS

The father returns from work and ignores his wife's request for assistance with the children. "You don't understand how difficult my day has been," he says. "I need to relax and watch TV. I'm right. You are wrong." That is the voice of Doe Chi. Any time you hear the words, "you don't understand how I feel," you are very likely hearing the voice of Doe Chi. Doe Chi ends up alone. Doe Chi blames others in order to release its own pain. "It's your fault" is a road sign along the Pa Doe pathway. That pathway leads to false humanness because it destroys harmony and peace.

5. STUCK ON FAILURE

"I truly have tried to change all my life, but it never works. I always stay the same." That is one of the many voices of Doe Chi. Doe Chi denies the Moo Doe principle: "You can change your own reality." If you have money problems: you created them, and you can change them. If you have relationship problems: you created them, and you can change them. In Gan is self-made. You can achieve In Gan by following principles, by tapping into the root of genuine power, by traveling the Chung Doe pathway.

6. STUCK ON SELF-PRIDE

"Why are you always criticizing me? Mind your own business." That is the voice of Doe Chi. Doe Chi rejects all criticism, rejects all suggestions. Doe Chi says, "I don't care how I look. I don't care how I live. I don't care about tomorrow." Doe Chi cannot see through the eyes of human beings nor understand the desire to help and improve them. Doe Chi is immune to love and friendship. Doe Chi has self-interest, but no self-knowledge. Doe Chi is blind to family and community bonds. Doe Chi has ears stopped up with self-pride. Doe Chi has eyes blinded with self-deception. Doe Chi has a heart hardened by ego of "defensive" self-pride .

THREE WAYS TO SILENCE DOE CHI

1. OPEN UP THE INVISIBLE EYE

The visible eye only sees the fluttering leaves and the swaying branches. It focuses on momentary likes and dislikes. The invisible eye sees the root and focuses on principles. Therefore, tap into the visible and invisible power. Choose In Gan as your goal—genuine humanness at its root center. Look for the good, the noble, the enduring—then you will find that the Correct will become visible to you each day. You will then know your true self and make an alliance with destiny as you journey along the Chung Doe pathway. Follow your heart. Follow the Moo Doe moral compass (True/Right/Correct). The clamor and noise of Doe Chi will give way to the quiet grandeur of deep power and lasting harmony.

2. Cultivate Genuine Friendship

The strongest sword is made of tempered steel that has been subjected to intense pressure and heat again and again until it is nearly indestructible. A genuine friend tempers your mind again and again until it becomes a sword of power. True friends would point out a negative quality to help you grow. If you do everything well, you are not learning. True friends help you build up your discipline. That is the principle of friendship. Be grateful for sincere, constructive criticism. Consider it an act of loyalty and love, an act of genuine friendship and compassion.

Suppose your spouse points out a deficiency in you. Maybe he or she doesn't like the clothes you are wearing. Understand where your spouse is coming from. What he or she is really saying is, "I am interested in you. I am interested in your well-being. I am your friend; therefore, I am telling you the way things are." Your spouse is acting on the principle of friendship. Look for this principle. Make the correct decision based on principle. What do you do? You improve! You respond to your friends! You are grateful.

True friendship is based on loyalty. Loyalty is a principle. It never changes. Likes and dislikes change with the moment. Your spouse is being loyal. You cannot buy loyalty; it must be earned. With loyalty, you will never be alone. In the business world they use "Choe Syeh." Choe Syeh is a process of gradually letting you see your faults. They tell you nine things you did right, then one thing you did wrong. True friends never use Choe Syeh. A true friend will tell you nine things you did wrong and one thing you did right.

That is genuine friendship. That is genuine loyalty. It says, "I am interested in helping you move forward along the Chung Doe pathway."

Do not expect grand gestures of approval from spouse or friends. Do not look for flowery compliments. Genuine friends show their approval in subtle and quiet ways. A special nod, a silent look. You learn the signals. Doe Chi is noisy and boisterous. Genuine friends do not cultivate Doe Chi, but rather deep and silent power. Marriage partners learn over the years to express their approval in invisible ways that come from the heart, not the tongue. With genuine friendship all around you, you will find that the clamor and show of Doe Chi will fade. In its place you will have the enduring power of the root.

3. Moving Meditation (Nae Gong)

You might say, "I have tried for years to change myself--my faults, my temper. But it doesn't work." The solution is to practice the exercise and movement techniques that have been handed down over the centuries by the grandmasters. There are many such steps to follow; the first is Nae Gong--moving meditation. Through moving meditation you will learn to look at yourself--not just your visible self, but your invisible self as well. Nae Gong is a mirror--not a visible mirror of the outer world, but a mirror that reveals the inner self, the invisible self. When you learn to look in that mirror, you will find the answer and you will change. There is greater knowledge of Nae Gong in the coming lessons.

GREAT STRENGTH OF
MIND AND BODY IN HARMONY
THAT IS THE VICTORY OF IN GAN—
HUMANNESS AT ITS ROOT CENTER

合心團結

*United
we stand,
divided
we fall.*

4

LEAVE BEHIND GOOD SEEDS

THE FOURTH STEP OF MOO DOE is to prepare to leave behind a legacy of good seeds for your children and coming generations. We come into the world with nothing, gather our material goods for a time, and then leave the world with nothing. To be remembered, we must leave behind a spiritual legacy of balance, harmony, peace, joy, and great internal and external power. This is the good fruit with the good seeds. These are the principles of creating such a legacy.

- Life is a challenge for good and for bad. It is your choice.
- The candle is needed in the darkest place. The darkest place is not "outside," but "inside" (near and within you).
- First illuminate yourself, and then illuminate the pathway for your family and loved ones.
- The legacy of Chung Doe is good seeds. The Legacy of Pa Doe is rotten fruit.
- Moving waters do not spoil, but stagnant waters do spoil.
- You can own material things, but should not let material things own you.
- Trust is born in the mind; trust changes. Faith is born in the heart; faith never changes.
- Faith is using your invisible eye to see yourself and your loved ones in a state of In Gan--humanness at its highest potential.
- Wisdom is making correct decisions in the spirit of faith.
- Only through faith and wisdom can you achieve the master key and pass it on.
- When you move along the Chung Doe pathway in faith and wisdom, your presence is felt there forever.

Light Upon the Face of Darkness

At noon, the grandmaster and his student were seated on a flat rock ledge near a flowing mountain stream. Far below them the citizens of the valley were cultivating their farms and gardens in the heat of the day. An eagle traced a spiral in the cloudless sky above the observers.

"How dark it is today?" asked the grandmaster. "I will now remove a candle from my bag and prepare to send illumination into the world." And he carefully lit a candle, shielding it from the breeze. Surprised, the student shielded his eyes from the sun and looked toward the grandmaster with anticipation.

"Where is the darkest place? Where is the candle needed most?" asked the grandmaster.

The student glanced around the area and replied. "Over there, perhaps, in the shadow of that oak tree?"

The grandmaster kept silent and the student added to his answer. "Or over there, where that cave leads into the mountain."

"Where is the closest, tightest place? That is where this candle is most needed," said the grandmaster.

The student was lost for words, so the grandmaster continued. "You look all around you for darkness. But you forget to look toward yourself. Beneath you, under you, between yourself and the rock where you sit--that is the darkest place. That is the closest, tightest place. That is where the candle is needed."

"The light of self-knowledge?" humbly asked the student.

"Yes," replied the grandmaster. "Look down there at all those workers in the valley. They labor to support their families, and that is a correct thing to do. But they labor in blindness. They do not see the darkness under their own feet. And when the time comes for them to die and go the way of all flesh, what do they leave behind?"

"Their farms, their homes," said the student.

"And after a time, who remembers them for these material things, what is the spiritual legacy they leave behind for their families?" questioned the grandmaster.

At this, the student could think of nothing to say and kept silent.

The grandmaster asked another question, "Are you hungry?"

"Oh, yes!" eagerly responded the student.

"What do you see here?" asked the grandmaster, pulling an object from a container in his bag. "Are you hungry for this?"

The student recoiled in horror at the sight of a piece of fruit decayed and rotten.

"Seok Eun Qua Eel," said the grandmaster.

"Rotten fruit! What for?" curiously echoed the student while distancing away from the rotten fruit.

"What for, indeed," repeated the grandmaster. "So many people leave a legacy for their families of rotten fruit. When they die, they leave behind them no good seeds for the next generation. Into the world they come with nothing. They gather up material goods for a time. And then they leave--with nothing. They see the world around them, but never themselves. They are quick to find fault with their neighbor, but overlook the darkness within themselves. They have no earnings."

"No earnings?" asked the student.

"There are only two types of riches for humans," replied the grandmaster. "Visible riches and invisible riches. We have visible riches for only a short time. But invisible riches last forever. The invisible riches come from being an honorable role model. Those are our earnings, our legacy. It is the invisible riches that are our good seed. This good seed will help others, who will in turn help still others. These invisible riches will multiply and grow. This is the principle of success in human life. These riches can be attained when people overcome the darkness within themselves."

"But how shall they change?" asked the student.

"By opening up their inner (invisible, spiritual) eye," explained the grandmaster. "Life is a challenge, for good or for bad. To see clearly the good path of Chung Doe requires looking in faith and wisdom with the invisible eye. Long before we were born, this path has existed. The visible eye too easily follows the material way of Pa Doe. The invisible eye follows the Moo Doe principle of True/Right/Correct along the Chung Doe pathway."

"How shall I prevent the fruit from spoiling?" asked the student.

"Movement," responded the grandmaster.

"Movement?" curiously repeated the student.

"Moving waters do not go stagnant, do not spoil," continued the grandmaster. "Moving waters are constantly being refreshed. See this stream. It remains fresh and pure by moving along its course of destiny toward the ocean."

"But Grandmaster," objected the student, "you once said that moving water speaks with the noisy voice of Doe Chi of selfishness."

"All of nature teaches the lesson you look for," explained the grandmaster. "Look carefully at this cascading stream. It does bubble and tumble. But along the cascade are many pools. Each pool is deep and calm. Nevertheless the water in each pool moves."

"The pools seem to be at rest," noted the student.

"But they move with invisible movement," described the grandmaster. "Like a human being agile with self-knowledge. Moving waters do not spoil, do not stagnate. Your life is like this deep moving water--'Hu Ru Run Mool.' Selfishness is rotten. Being drunk with material things is rotten. Moving water endures. A spiritual legacy lives on forever. What do you see up there?"

Looking upward, the student replied, "I see the eagle circling."

"The eagle moves slowly, gracefully, surely," explained the grandmaster. "The eagle teaches 'In Gan'--humanness at its root center. Between the clouds and the sky is the realm of In Gan. Look for yourself there in that place. Look with the invisible eye. Leave behind you a legacy of balance, harmony, peace, joy, and great internal and external power. Be such a human being. When such a human being walks along the pathway, his presence is felt there forever. That is the spiritual legacy. That is the good fruit with the good seed."

Then, the grandmaster handed the lit candle to the student and said, "It is your destiny to send illumination into the world. That is your hunger. That is your mission. Are you truly hungry?"

The student did not dare to respond to this question and kept silent.

The grandmaster smiled and continued saying, "There are two hungers: the invisible hunger for the enduring spiritual legacy, and the visible hunger for essential food. Come, let us go down and pick some fresh fruit in the valley."

The student was relieved. He smiled. He understood. "How can I be more like you, Grandmaster?" he respectfully asked.

"In the next lesson you will learn," calmly replied the grandmaster.

THE LESSON

Life is a challenge for good and for bad. When you follow the Chung Doe pathway, the outcome is good fruit--good seed for the next generation. When you follow the Pa Doe pathway, the outcome is rotten fruit—of no value for the coming generation. Rotten fruit breaks down and returns to the earth to be recycled for the good of a more worthy, unfolding of life later on. The good seed endures and spreads hope to the next generation.

Moo Doe principles have been passed down over the centuries as a bond to preserve the family. A human being who has come to know his or her true self understands that one of life's purposes is to pass on to the children a good name and a good role model of how to achieve balance, harmony, peace, and great power. A good role model follows the Moo Doe moral compass of True/Right/Correct in order to become In Gan, which is the highest form of humanness and humanness at its root center. In Gan loves light. On the contrary, Keum Soo is the animal side of humanness and it loves darkness. In Gan sees the light in others and feels the drive to help them find more light. But, Keum Soo sees the darkness in others and feels the drive to expand the darkness.

How do you feel? You can touch yourself and know that you exist. Are you light or darkness? Is there darkness in you that needs to be filled with illumination? With your visible eye, you can see your hands, your body, and your visible self. But can you see the invisible self? Can you open the invisible eye and see the heart, the true self, and the root of your being? If you can see the invisible self with the invisible eye, then you see the legacy that you will leave behind when you die.

HOW WILL YOU BE REMEMBERED?

If you were to die tomorrow, how would you be remembered? As a successful business person, doctor, lawyer, or some other profession with a fancy title? Would you be remembered as a person that taught their children and others the way of honor and peace? How will your family be affected when you die? What will they think of you? They have the visible things you have gathered together. But what kind of enduring legacy are the visible things? They can bring ease and comfort, but they fade away like the petals of a flower. The good seeds are: a good name and enduring lessons of courage, power, character, and service.

We come into the world with nothing. For a time we gather together our visible things. But these do not endure. When we die, we take nothing with us. Many humans become prisoners of material things. They boast with Doe Chi voices about their power and might, their possessions. But when Death comes to call on them in their homes, their strength passes away like the leaves in autumn, and when they blow out the candle and go away with Death, they leave behind darkness and rotten fruit (Seok Eun Qua Eel).

Open up your invisible eye. What do you see yourself giving to your family? What Moo Doe lessons do you act out for them on the stage of life? How are you teaching them to use the compass of True/Right/Correct? What light do you shed on the pathway your family is to follow? You can give them material gifts and comforts to add variety and joy to life; but these will fade. The spiritual gifts that give self-respect and joy of service—these will endure. You can own material things, but do not let material things own you.

PRINCIPLE OR HEART?

How should you look at your children, your family members? You can look at them in two ways: with heart and with principle. When you look at them with principle, you must look at them as if they were stones or trees. No matter what they say in return, principle never changes for them. Principle is deaf to opinion and blind to objections.

When you look at your family members with your heart, you look at them for what they are: growing, beautiful human beings who are becoming In Gan, humanness at its root center.

There is a time for principle. There is a time for heart. Many never look with principle upon their children, and thus they curse them and deprive them of light. Many never look with heart upon their children, and thus they curse them and deprive them of faith. But to look with both principle and heart is to leave behind a legacy of wisdom and faith--the good seed of balance, harmony, power, peace, and joy.

You give a child an apple. That is a gift of the heart. The apple gives momentary joy and keeps the child satisfied for an hour. Then the child asks for more. So you give the child a cartload of apples. But that is neither an act of the heart, nor an act of principle. It is folly. The act of principle is to teach the child to grow apple trees. The child may resist learning the work of growing apple trees, but principle is unyielding to excuses. The parent sees through the invisible eye the child growing up and being able to enjoy apples for a lifetime. The heart is happy over this view, and principle is preserved on behalf of the child. The heart and principle working together--that is wisdom, that is the correct decision.

MOVING WATER

Where does the good seed flourish? Near flowing streams of deep, clam water. Moving water (Hu Ru Run Mool) does not spoil, does not stagnant. Where is the moving water? Truly, it is in those families where principle and heart combine to teach togetherness, love, selfless service, and the joy of staying strong and resolute on the good pathway. Living and caring in such a family, you leave behind your presence, which shall never, ever depart.

THE MASTER KEY

The master key is faith plus wisdom. Faith is using your invisible eye to see yourself and your loved ones in a state of In Gan--humanness in its highest potential. Wisdom is making correct choices in the spirit of faith and hope. By way of contrast, trust is a product of the mind. Trust can change from time to time because it is a way of thinking. Trust seems deep, but that is an illusion. Beware of the temptation to place your trust in worldly institutions or worldly guides. Trust is heavy and cannot rise on the spiritual wings of faith and wisdom. Trust is deep water that is not moving. Faith and wisdom are deep water that is moving. Moving water never spoils.

Look around you at all the buildings in the community. Each door takes a different key. How many keys would you need to open all those buildings? There are many keys on each human being's key rings. But if you had the master key, then one is enough. Look around you at all the challenges of life. Each is different. Each calls for you in a different voice. But if you respond with faith and wisdom, you need only one key. The master key is faith and wisdom. Leave such a key behind for your loved ones. That is the good seed for which you will never be forgotten. Life is a challenge for good or for bad. You have the choice.

GREAT STRENGTH OF MIND AND BODY IN HARMONY: THOSE ARE THE GOOD SEEDS

Determination

5

SEEK THE FACE OF HONOR

THE FIFTH STEP OF MOO DOE is to seek the face of honor. Honor means living in such a way that you pass on the good seeds to your children and the coming generations. Honor means preserving the connection to the root, the source of enduring strength and vitality. Honor is driven by love and sustained through respect. Honor produces Chung Doe fruits of harmony, balance, peace, and joy. Honor overcomes the Pa Doe forces of greed, envy, selfishness, anger, and prejudice. These are the principles to follow to seek the face of honor.

- The central power behind honor is love.
- The central fruits of honor are harmony, balance, peace, and joy.
- The central meaning of honor is to pass the good seeds on to the coming generations.
- In Gan has one face, the face of honor. Finding your one "true" face is humanness at its root center.
- Honor is the mountain; the mountain does not change.
- What has a thousand faces, and yet no face? Keum Soo—many false faces, and no true face.
- A mask lives only for the present; a face of honor lives forever.
- Without honor, there are no true friends. With honor, friends are legion.
- To be connected to the root is the principle of life; to be separated from the root is death.
- You lift others to the Chung Doe level through the power of respect.
- Go with destiny by changing your reality.
- Chung Doe pays a thousand-fold, for the good seeds spread without end.

The One Face of Honor

The sun was just rising as the grandmaster and his student began their descent down the hill toward the village. In the distance, the rosy glow of morning touched the snowy peak of the mountain.

"How beautiful?" remarked the student. "The mountain presents many faces. Sometimes pink like this morning. Sometimes red in the evening. Sometimes gray in the moonlight. Sometimes black against the starry sky."

"Many expressions. One face," replied the grandmaster.

"How so?" asked the student.

"Mountain is mountain," responded the grandmaster. "Always the same. Mountain has the face of honor. What face do you have?"

The student silently touched his own cheek.

"Look at me, what do you see?" asked the grandmaster.

"I see the face of wisdom," replied the student.

"And?" quickly asked the grandmaster.

"The face of kindness," responded the student.

"And?" again asked the grandmaster.

"The face of peace," responded the student.

"And?" again asked the grandmaster.

"The face of power," responded the student.

"How many faces do you see?" questioned the grandmaster.

"Four," answered the student, somewhat bewildered.

"Count again," insisted the grandmaster.

The student understood the principle and said, "Grandmaster, I see one face--the face of honor."

The grandmaster smiled and said, "It is very important to have face."

"I too have face," added the student.

"We shall see," remarked the grandmaster.

By now, the two had entered the village. Many people were rushing about at the start of the workday. The grandmaster pointed his finger at a bench beneath an oak tree near the market square. There they sat down to observe the people.

"So many faces, do you see their faces?" asked the grandmaster.

"Yes, I see many faces," confirmed the student.

"Many visible faces," commented the grandmaster, "but in many cases their true faces are invisible--hidden by the masks of Keum Soo."

"Masks?" questioned the student. "I see no masks."

"The key is the eyes," said the grandmaster. "The eyes are the windows of the true face. See that woman over there holding her newborn child? What do you see in her eyes?"

"I see peace," responded the student.

"Yes," agreed the grandmaster, "she is a traveler on the Chung Doe pathway. She aspires to a face of honor. The face of honor has eyes of peace. She has a vision of leaving good seeds behind for her child. What do you see over there?"

The student looked in the direction of a villager in fancy clothing, strutting proudly across the square with nose high in the air. "I see a wealthy man," commented the student, "perhaps the wealthiest in the village. Look, he is giving a coin to that beggar."

"You see a mask of Keum Soo," responded the grandmaster, "his true face is not visible."

"He seems rather sure of himself," observed the student.

"He deceives himself," said the grandmaster. "He thinks he has the face of power and wealth, but that is a mask, a mask of Keum Soo. He thinks he can wear the face of charity, but that too is a mask, for he has gained his wealth by stealing from others. His eyes are the eyes of greed. He pretends to wear the face of honor, but in fact he has no face at all. He travels the Pa Doe pathway. He leaves behind no good seeds."

"Can such people change their masks to fit the occasion?" asked the student.

"Keum Soo has many faces, many masks," responded the grandmaster. "Wearing masks always has consequences. Masks can cause great damage to the individual and to others. Masks leave no good seed. In Gan has one face, the face of honor. A mask lives only for the present. A face of honor lives forever. Finding your one 'true' face--that is humanness at its root center."

Just then, two young men walked up and sat down on an adjacent bench to talk. One wore a red shirt, the other blue.

"Listen carefully," said the grandmaster to his student.

"How good to see you again," said the man in the red shirt to his companion. "I missed you during your trip. We were always such close friends."

After the two had exchanged warm compliments and renewed their friendship for a few minutes, the man in blue bid his friend farewell and walked away to enter a nearby shop.

"They wear the face of friendship and honor," believed the student.

"Wait and see," instructed the grandmaster.

Presently, a young woman walked up and sat down next to the man in red.

"I noticed your friend has returned from his trip," she said.

"Yes," responded the man in red.

"I often wondered about him," she continued.

"Always so happy and cheerful he is. I think it is all an act. None of us ever really trusted him."

"Exactly," agreed the man in red, "he always had it so easy. Always the lucky one (man). Always thought he was so good. What a pain he is!"

The student looked over at the grandmaster in surprise, and the grandmaster asked, "What do you see?"

"I understand now," replied the student. "The man in red has two faces."

"Only two?" asked the grandmaster. "Where there are two, there are more. Here is a riddle: What has a thousand faces and yet no face?"

"Keum Soo," answered the student.

"Yes," confirmed the grandmaster, "Keum Soo faces are masks only. There is no true face there, only self-deception. Remember, having no face is having no honor. Without honor, there are no friends; with honor, friends are legion."

Moments later, the young man in red stood up, said good-bye to the young woman, and disappeared into the crowd. Soon the young man in blue returned, holding a bundle of fresh fruit.

"Hello," he said to the young woman, "it's good to see you again. I was just talking to..."

"Yes," she interrupted. "He left for an appointment, thank heavens."

"What do you mean?" asked the man in blue.

"What a snake he is!" she exclaimed. "No good at all."

"Stop!" said the young man. "He is my friend, and I will hear no wrong said about him."

"Some friend," she replied. "You should have heard the bad things he said about you behind your back."

"If that is the case," responded the young man, "then I would prefer to hear those things from him directly. As his friend, I owe him that much. He remains my friend until he proves otherwise."

Then, the young man in blue nodded goodbye and departed quickly.

"What do you see now?" asked the grandmaster.

"I see the man in blue has face," replied the student, "he is an honorable man. The others have masks, but no face. Face is honor. I too want the face of honor."

"And if you have such a face," asked the grandmaster, "when will you show it?"

"I will show that same face always," assured the student.

"That is correct," said the grandmaster. "You will show the face of honor to your friends, to your family, to everyone. That is the face you will pass on to your next generation, the face of honor. You will do this because you are the mountain, and the mountain does not change. You are deep moving water that remains fresh and pure. You are the eagle that circles high above the clouds. You are the traveler below on the Chung Doe pathway."

"Grandmaster, how can I be like you?" sincerely asked the student.

"Open the invisible eye," calmly said the grandmaster. "See your 'true' self unfolding. Go with destiny by changing your reality."

"How can I change my reality?" asked the student, puzzled.

"With the next lesson, we shall see," replied the grandmaster, who was already striding away from the crowd.

THE LESSON

The wisdom of the ages, passed down from generation to generation, teaches the fundamental truth that all things are connected. The principle behind this is that the strength comes from the root, for the root endures. From the root flows the life of the individual, family, and community. To be connected to the root is the principle of life. To be separated from the root is death. Therefore, the highest good in life is to follow the way of connectedness successfully and pass on the good seeds to the coming generations.

The individual who is a role model of connectedness on the Chung Doe pathway is a human being of honor. Honor is the central principle of Moo Doe morals. The central meaning of honor is to pass the good seeds on to your children and coming generations. The central power behind honor is love--love of your family and your children, your community and all human beings. The central fruits of honor are harmony, balance, peace, and joy.

The opposite of honor is dishonor. The greatest dishonor in life is to withhold good seeds from your family and coming generations—either through action or lack of action—with the result that they are denied a good name, harmony, balance, peace, joy, and great external and internal power. Such a denial breaks the connection and brings a separation from the root.

The primary motivating force behind dishonor is hate. How is it possible for humans to hate their own family, their own children, and other human beings?

Those humans who love the fruits of the Pa Doe pathway more than family and others, can be said to hate family and others because these are sacrificed for visible things, worldly glory, and self-pride. The quest for such things is the vocation of Doe Chi--being drunk with one's (your) own thoughts and words.

Many humans, however, seek honor without connectedness, without love. Instead, they seek honor in visible things. Moreover, they seek honor in tearing down rather than building up, breaking apart rather than connecting, serving self rather than serving others. They have no face because they have no honor. Instead, they wear a false face, a mask. In fact, they have many masks, one for each human they meet, one for each occasion in life. They are Keum Soo, the animal side of humanness. Keum Soo has a thousand faces, and yet no face.

By way of contrast, In Gan has only one "true" face and no masks. In Gan is the highest form of humanness and humanness at its root center. In Gan has the same face of honor for all occasions, and for all human beings, and for all time. To find your own true face of honor is to bring about connectedness, to connect with the coming generations through the good seed. Thus In Gan comes about through love, while Keum Soo comes about through hate.

THE THREE ZEROES

HEAD   STOMACH   FEET

A principle of life is: You are born and that is why you must die. The visible aspect of life is three zeros which correlate to the head, the stomach, and the feet.

The first zero, the head, signifies the sky. You are born into this world with nothing. The second zero, the stomach, signifies the earth. During your life you temporarily own what you have. Life is a test to determine whether good seeds or bad seeds were left behind for the next generation. The third zero, the feet, signifies death. Once you die, you leave with nothing. Your spirit came from God and must return to be judged accordingly whether good or bad.

Two Kinds of Hate

There are two kinds of hate: hate based on greed, and hate based on ignorance. To look for the easy way in life is the way of greed, the way of Keum Soo. That form of hate says, "These others have what I want. Therefore, I must take it from them. To take it from them, I must declare them to have no value. Since they have no value, I can hate them, and dispossess them." But such is the voice of Doe Chi. It is spoken by a mask, by someone with no true self. It is self-deception because it masks the truth. The truth is that such a dishonorable human has hate for him/herself because he or she has been disconnected and dismissed from his or her own potential greatness. Those who deny themselves the goal of In Gan—the highest potential of human beings—will hate themselves. To hate oneself is a tragic predicament, because it leads to death and to "rotten fruit."

The other form of hate is based on ignorance--not knowing your true self, or worse, not knowing that you do not know. Hiding behind the mask of ignorance is a form of self-hatred, because it says, "I do not know my true self, and I am not worth knowing. What I do not know, I cannot love. Therefore, I must hate myself. That is why I must wear the mask of ignorance--to cover the shame of the truth." Such an individual can pass down no good seeds. Such an individual is broken off from the true root. Such an individual has no honor, and therefore no face. Thus, it is urgent to know your true self and to find the face of honor.

HOW TO FIND HONOR

When you are on the Chung Doe pathway, you find honor by lifting others up to the Chung Doe level to be your companions. The parent lifts the child. The teacher lifts the student. The friend lifts the friend. How do you lift? Through the power of respect. True respect means honoring the light in others. You honor the light in others by helping them connect to the root of strength and purpose. Respect means being a good role model. True respect means planting seeds of harmony, balance, peace, and joy.

There is no respect in forcing others to change, or in doing for them what they should correctly learn to do for themselves. That would deprive them of the opportunity to learn the principle of True/Right/Correct. Rather, respect means teaching others to open their invisible eye and see themselves in their true light as In Gan--the highest form of humanness. When they see themselves in this true light, they desire to choose the Correct, for the fruits of the Chung Doe pathway become sweet and delicious to them.

Honor means respecting others in their place of service, in the role they perform for the good of all. Consider the house. The main beam of the house supports the whole house. When the window does not fit securely, and the winds and rains come in, the main beam does not leave its place to become the window. If that were to happen, the whole house would fall. Similarly, the door does not become the wall, nor the wall the ceiling. Rather, all are connected together. Each plays its essential role. Likewise, in the family, the parents support the whole, but still show respect for each child by allowing him or her to learn duty and honor in playing a role suited to their age and ability. The parents respect the light in each other and in each child, and therefore cultivate balance, sharing, love, and mutual respect.

INVISIBLE HARM

What is it that is missing in our modern world? It is the fundamental sense of connectedness. The family is under siege from the forces of separation, of breaking apart, of being disconnected from the root. Honor grows with great difficulty in the rocky seedbed of material excess. Respect struggles to survive in an atmosphere of greed and selfishness. The Pa Doe pathway is barren and devoid of growth. Doe Chi winds dry out the parched earth and suppress the tender shoots. But the greatest harm from being disconnected from the root is invisible, because it happens with in. Being separated from the root brings internal doubt and insecurity. Doubt and insecurity cover the face of the true self and create hunger for external masks.

The modern world is ablaze with the grotesque masks of Keum Soo--the masks of greed, envy, selfishness, anger, and prejudice. These masks stare outwardly with the eyes of hate and destruction, but the hate and destruction also stay within to scar the soul. Greed consumes the heart a little at a time, until the heart dies. Envy kills self-confidence and initiative with the flattering lie that what others have earned you can seize with no effort on your part. Selfishness will steal another's honor; but the selfish individual really steals only from oneself by denying self-worth and potential. Anger destroys balance and harmony and renders inoperative the Moo Doe moral compass of True/Right/Correct. Prejudice violates love by stealing away the worth and respect of others.

All of these masks hide the real villain--hatred of self. Hatred of self is the result of separation from the root, of disconnectedness. When you lose the connection, you lose sight of the true self. When you lose the connection, the invisible mirror is clouded over with doubt and ignorance. When you lose the connection, you leave nothing behind but rotten fruit for the coming generation. But it need not be so. All life is a challenge for good or for bad. You can choose for yourself.

THE INVISIBLE HUNGER

There is a fundamental hunger within each human being for connectedness. Each human being feels incomplete without a bridge to close friends. But in a world dominated by the spirit of Pa Doe, how shall a human choose friends correctly? How shall we satisfy the invisible hunger for friendship and still have security? Throughout history, it has always been known that humans fall into two broad categories: those who act as human beings, and those who act as wild animals. How can you expect human treatment and friendship from a wild animal? If you get too close to a wild animal, it may bite you. Blame cannot be placed on the animal, because it was your choice to get into that position.

Similarly, you have the choice of which humans will be close to you. The Moo Doe moral compass of True/Right/Correct is a powerful tool for correctly choosing friends. Look within yourself and open the invisible eye to view your prospective friends in the illumination of eternal principle. True friendship is based on a mutual kinship rooted in principle, rooted in a shared vision of traveling together along the Chung Doe pathway leading to In Gan, the highest form of humanness.

Such companionship is a bond not to be severed by hardship and difficult challenges in life. True friendship is more than shallow talk and words; it is deeply rooted, and demonstrated through the actions of loyalty, trust, togetherness, honor, and mutual respect. True friendship satisfies the invisible hunger within. True friendship is a food. Sometimes sweet, sometimes sour—but it is always savored with enduring loyalty. When the friendship is sweetened by the joys of life, you swallow it as something smooth. When the friendship is soured by the pains of life, you do not spit it out as something rough and jagged. You take the smooth and the rough both, because true friendship is togetherness, no matter what happens. With true friendship, you are never alone. That is the way to success. That is the moral principle of friendship.

True Friendship with Complete Trust

There is no true friendship without complete trust. Friendship without trust is a dawn with no sun, a fire with no warmth. How unfortunate it is in today's world that humans feel they cannot trust each other. By withholding trust, they feel they are shielding themselves from harm. But the invisible hunger for connectedness can never be satisfied by withholding trust. Those who withhold trust are harming themselves within. They are feeding on their own self-doubt; they are nourishing themselves on their own emptiness. Therefore, they are starving to death by not learning how to trust other human beings. They go nowhere and their efforts end in failure.

Those who waste precious time learning how to live their lives mistrusting, should instead spend that time learning how to place trust correctly in other human beings. Throughout history, the lesson has been passed down from one generation to the next that no good fruit can be harvested without the giving and placing of trust. You must use the pure "open" (spiritual) eye to place complete trust correctly in others. Trust does not follow the shrill Doe Chi voices of greed and selfishness, or the shallow fickleness of Gan Sa. Trust follows the deep, still voice of enduring principle along the Chung Doe pathway.

When you use the pure "open" eye to place trust correctly, your confidence in your correct judgment and your trust in yourself will grow and mature. Using the correct form of trust leads to success in life. This complete trust is the way of honor. Honor dictates that if you question a true friend, examine the question carefully from all sides before making a judgment.

Spiritual Trust

Trust is a mirror that reflects spiritual truth. Most, if not all, religion and spiritual belief systems are grounded in both trust and faith. Hence, consider these principles of the Chung Doe pathway to have spiritual truth and faith.

- The pathway of trust and faith was here long before you were born and will remain long after you die. Choosing this pathway is a key choice for success in life.
- A life without trust and faith is a life not aligned with the spiritual, and thus not aligned with your spiritual beliefs.

- A life without trust and faith may be rich in visible things, but poor in invisible (spiritual) things.
- A life with trust and faith may be rich in both kinds of wealth: visible things in sufficiency, and invisible (spiritual) things in abundance— balance, harmony, pure relationships, true friendships, peace, and joy.
- Do we not teach our children what is up as well as down, in as well as out, and night as well as day? Why then do we so seldom teach them the correct way to trust others, rather than just how to be constantly in a state of self-defense?
- Walls will tumble, shields will rust, and armies will fade away. The only secure way to protect our children forever is to teach them to be their own guard through pure (correct) trust.
- To know how to trust correctly is to learn to see through the pure "open" (spiritual) eye.

THE GARDENER

Knowing your true self is a choice. Like the gardener, you can clear away the weeds of doubt and insecurity before they choke off the growth of the tender plants. You can cultivate the soil of honor. You can channel the waters of respect. You can nourish the plants with faith and hope, looking toward the harvest. You can preserve the connection to the root. You can grow the good seeds to pass on to your children and the coming generations. You can see the true self clearly in your invisible mirror. You can choose the Chung Doe pathway.

If you have strayed from the main path, you can recover to the high ground. If you have wandered onto the Pa Doe pathway, you can repair the internal harm and reclaim the task of cultivating the good seeds for the coming generations. If you have allowed material things to possess you, rather than you possessing them for the good of others, you can change your reality. You can discard the Keum Soo masks and silence the voice of Doe Chi. You can glow with the light of honor and shine with the light of In Gan.

But do not delay. The gardener knows that the growing season is short. The harvest is near. Pa Doe demands double the price. Every day lost is two days spent—one wasted on the wrong path, another required to catch up on the right path. On the other hand, Chung Doe pays a thousand-fold, for the good seeds spread without end, season after season, until destiny brings you and the coming generations to the top of the mountain, to In Gan--the highest form of humanness. That is the correct way. It is up to you.

GREAT STRENGTH OF MIND AND BODY IN HARMONY: THAT COMES WHEN YOU FIND THE FACE OF HONOR

A strong will

6

CHANGE YOUR REALITY

THE SIXTH STEP OF MOO DOE is to learn to change your own reality and thus assure your progress along the Chung Doe pathway toward the realization of your highest potential (In Gan). Those who allow themselves to be imprisoned (surrounded by invisible walls) by their own reality follow the Pa Doe pathway to isolation and disconnectedness. As Moo Doe masters have taught, only through the exquisite exercises and movements of Nae Gong can a human be fully connected with the unlimited natural energy, and thus accrue to themselves and others the vitality and healing influences that await those who move resolutely in alignment with destiny. These are guidelines to follow to change your reality.

- You can change your reality. That is always your choice.
- First learn, then earn.
- Knowledge sees visible things; wisdom sees invisible things.
- You can gain knowledge from others, but you must gain wisdom by yourself.
- Nae Gong is the true energy of internal strength.
- The secrets of Nae Gong are the wings of wisdom.
- By giving of your "true" self, you find your true self. Open your invisible eye, follow the Moo Doe moral compass of True/Right/Correct, and use Nae Gong to connect with unlimited natural energy--these are the tools of destiny.

The key to happiness is to earn by sharing with and serving others. In return, those whom you have served shall serve you.

The Young Eagle's First Flight

There was silence in the valley, interrupted only by the occasional cooing of a mourning dove. The grandmaster and his student were walking silently along the path that led through a grove of trees.

"Mind and body off balance," suddenly spoke the grandmaster.

"It is true that I have an uneasy feeling in my stomach, but how did you know? I am walking normally. I am talking normally," replied the student, startled.

"I know through wisdom. Wisdom sees hidden things in the eyes, in the face," said the grandmaster.

"I do not want to be sick," said the student.

"Look at that small tree," instructed the grandmaster, "what do you see?"

"Many leaves," replied the student.

"Many leaves, yes," agreed the grandmaster. "But look carefully at the colors. A few of the leaves are a different shade--much browner. These leaves are sick, ready to drop. The others are healthy. Life is not much different than that. Some stay connected, some not."

"To be truthful," responded the student, "I have not felt very well since we ate rabbit yesterday. Really, I am very sick. How can I be healed?"

"Change your reality," replied the grandmaster.

"My reality?" questioned the student.

"This sickness is your reality. You can change your reality. That is always your choice," answered the grandmaster.

"How do I do that?" asked the student, boggled.

At that, the grandmaster reached into the folds of his robe and removed a small sprig of green and said, "You should gather this herb and use it. That way you will learn knowledge and begin to earn wisdom."

"Where do I find this herb?" asked the student.

The grandmaster turned and looked off into the distance toward the white peak on the horizon and replied, "Up there, on the summit of the mountain."

"You mean you want me to go up there and find it?" questioned the student.

"Do you want to be well again?" counter questioned the grandmaster.

"Yes," immediately answered the student.

"Then learn to change your reality," said the grandmaster.

"But Grandmaster, there is a raging river between here and that mountain," responded the student, boggled again.

"Yes," agreed the grandmaster.

"And Grandmaster, the summit is surrounded by treacherous cliffs," added the student.

"Yes," said the grandmaster in a relaxed voice.

"And Grandmaster, I have no knowledge of how to climb those cliffs," again added the student, worried.

"Yes," again replied the grandmaster.

"And Grandmaster, there are dangerous animals that live in that region," again added the student.

"Yes," again said the grandmaster. "Take this herb and match it exactly. Life is a challenge for good or for bad. When you learn to change your reality for the good, you have the opportunity to earn wisdom."

The student swallowed hard and felt the ache in the pit of his stomach, however, he had faith and boldly said, "I will go." Then, he bowed in reverence and began his journey.

The next day, toward evening, the grandmaster heard a knock on the door of his cottage. It was the student, bent over with exhaustion and sickness, his clothing torn, his arms and hands bruised and scratched. But he beamed with satisfaction as he pulled a thatch of greenery from his shirt. "Here, the herb," he said.

The grandmaster took a sample of it in his left hand and the original in his right hand. He brought them close together until they touched. "It is correct," he said. "They match. Now go and change your reality."

The student was confused and asked, "But how shall I use this herb? Shall I just eat it?"

"In the Am Ja, make tea," replied the grandmaster.

"But I don't know how," said the student.

"That is your reality," replied the grandmaster, "so change your..."

"Reality," interrupted the student.

The grandmaster smiled and turned back to the cottage. As he closed the door, he said, "First learn, then earn. To change your reality, start from the beginning.

Remember, you are not a brown leaf on the tree. Stay connected."

Bewildered, the student walked down the pathway to the Am Ja where he fumbled first with one utensil and then with another. Finally, he succeeded in crushing the herbs and placing them in boiling water to steep. Then he poured a cup of tea and sipped it slowly.

Within a short period he could feel fingers of warmth and power moving through his body. Soon he felt complete relief. Running back to the cottage, he once more knocked on the door.

The grandmaster appeared and asked, "Yes?"

"Thank you, Grandmaster. I am greatly relieved," said the student.

"Do not thank me," said the grandmaster, "thank yourself. Now you know in this situation how to change your reality."

"How did this sickness happen?" wondered the student. "I am young and so strong--never sick until now. Why did you not get sick from the rabbit?"

"All of your life you have been building Wae Gong," said the grandmaster, "never Nae Gong. Wae Gong is external strength. Nae Gong is great internal strength."

"I did not know about internal strength, Grandmaster," said the student, intrigued.

"Only very few know Nae Gong," replied the grandmaster in solemn tones. "Nae Gong is the key to great internal balance and power. With Nae Gong, you are capable of always winning and beating any natural sickness. When you learn this, you will be able to help many others to be stronger. That is earning."

The student fell silent at the sound of these words and the grandmaster continued, "Nae Gong is the true Moo Doe internal strength. With Nae Gong, you and the mountain are truly one (existence, energy)."

The student turned his eyes again toward the summit from which he had just returned and continued to carefully listen.

"First learn, then earn," explained the grandmaster. "Through the herb you can earn relief for the moment. Through the journey, you can earn the secret of life forever."

"It is good," said the student, but his eyes expressed something else.

"You have a question," observed the grandmaster.

"Yes," replied the student, gathering his courage. "I was sick. I was helpless. Why did you not help me more with the climb and with the tea?"

The grandmaster put his arm around the shoulder of the student and said: "When the young eagle first flies, it flies alone. The parents are nearby, not too close and not too far away. I was behind you all the way. You can gain knowledge from others, but wisdom you must gain by yourself. Wisdom is greater than knowledge. Knowledge divides; wisdom connects. I will not always be with you. Therefore, the time for you to start gaining wisdom is now."

The student reverently bowed his head and said, "Grandmaster, Nae Gong is deep."

"The secrets of Nae Gong are the wings of wisdom," elaborated the grandmaster. "With Nae Gong, you speed the journey toward In Gan--the highest form of humanness."

"Why have you not taught me Nae Gong before?" asked the student.

"You were not ready yet," responded the grandmaster. "But it is now time to teach you the special movements that will connect you, that will make you one (existence, energy) with the mountain. You will learn to work with nature--with wind, fire, and water--the source of great internal strength. Once you have learned how to connect in this way, you can use Nae Gong to heal many others and help them, in turn, to gain great internal strength. First you learn, then you earn. To earn through service to others is the key to happiness."

"And I will be able to help others heal themselves of illness, Grandmaster?" wondered the student.

"Yes," confirmed the grandmaster. "Once you have learned Nae Gong, you will begin to earn the good seed to pass on to your children and many others, including coming generations. The good seed is balance, harmony, peace, joy, and great external and internal strengths."

"When do we begin?" excitedly asked the student.

"With the next lesson," calmly replied the grandmaster.

THE LESSON

Over the centuries Moo Doe wisdom has taught that life is a challenge for good or for bad. Good or bad is within each of us. We can choose to follow the one path or the other. If we follow the Pa Doe pathway (wrong path), we move in the direction of imbalance, selfishness, shallowness of character, isolation, and lack of integrity. If we follow the Chung Doe pathway (right path), we move in the direction of harmony, balance, service, togetherness, and integrity.

Many humans do not clearly see that life offers them this grand choice. Instead, they see themselves as victims of their surroundings and circumstances. They see themselves defined by their own reality, rather than having the power to define their own reality.

REALITY

Reality is what we see and believe concerning our surroundings and ourselves. Many humans believe reality to be something fixed, something that holds them back. For them, reality is a prison. They stare each day at the four walls of their reality and feel locked in. They see bars on the doors and windows. They see nothing but restraints to their progress, with no way to escape.

But there is another way to look at reality. You can look at your reality as something that you can change. You can see genuine opportunity at every turn. You can see reality not as a prison, but as an environment that is dynamic, challenging, and full of choices. You can see reality as a condition of growth and improvement. By making correct choices in this kind of dynamic reality, you move toward In Gan--humanness at its root center and the highest form of humanness.

On the other hand, if humans feel caged in by their reality, and allow it to control them, they do not grow spiritually, but remain at an animal level of existence called Keum Soo, having neither hope for a better future nor the wisdom to create it. Such humans lose sight of their true self, and hide behind the masks of greed, envy, and blame. Since they have lost sight of their own potential, they cover their insecurity by blaming their misfortunes and shortcomings on others or on circumstances or both. Such Pa Doe followers are easy to spot, for they boast of personal strength while tearing others down. They take delight in gossip and accusation. They spend vast amounts of energy making up excuses, rather than using this same energy to change their reality for the better. The problem is: They don't know how to change their reality.

HOW TO CHANGE YOUR REALITY

There are three steps for changing your reality.

1. **Open** your invisible eye and see your true self as In Gan, having the potential of unlimited progress. With one glance of your invisible eye, prison walls dissolve and restraints disappear. Excuses pass away like dry leaves in a fire, like dust in the wind, like froth on the waves of the sea. You see yourself with choices for good and for

bad, and you choose the good, the Chung Doe pathway (good principle).

2. **Follow** the Moo Doe moral compass of True/Right/Correct. By making correct decisions on a daily basis, you learn and earn. By choosing to improve yourself--no matter what your circumstances or station in life--you lift yourself up in correct ways to serve others. Through continual movement (learning and earning), you gain in understanding and wisdom. You move forward like the deep waters of a great river flowing to the ocean. You begin to grow the invisible seeds to pass on to your family and to your community as a legacy of love.

3. **Go** with nature as the source of great energy. Connect with this natural flow of energy through the powerful exercises and beautiful movements of Nae Gong. Changing your reality requires not only external strength, but great internal strength. These exercises and movements of Nae Gong have been passed down for centuries as the means to connect with natural energy--the power of vitality in life. It is this connection that promotes health and pours extraordinary healing influences over the participant.

These three steps--open your invisible eye, follow the Moo Doe moral compass, and use Nae Gong to connect with unlimited natural energy--are tools of destiny. By using these tools, you accelerate your progress along the

Chung Doe pathway and rise on the wings of wisdom. Through wisdom you earn your way on the journey of life. Earning your way means serving others as you serve yourself. By bringing the natural energy into your body, you gain tremendous power to do good. By giving of your true self, you find your true self. Therefore, first learn to improve yourself and change your reality, then earn by serving others. By earning, you cultivate the good seeds to pass on to your family and the coming generations.

MOO DOE TRIANGLE OF CHANGE

We can summarize and enhance these thoughts by studying the following diagram.

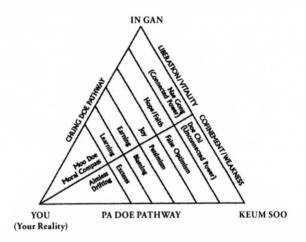

(The triangle is what you see in the invisible mirror)

The Moo Doe Triangle of Change shows what you see in the invisible mirror--a clear perspective of your choices in life. Place yourself at the bottom left corner of the triangle. This is your present position, your "reality." Life is a challenge for good or for bad. By following the Pa Doe pathway, you move toward confinement and weakness, eventually becoming Keum Soo--the animal side of humanness. By following the Chung Doe pathway, you move toward liberation and vitality, eventually becoming In Gan--the highest form of humanness and humanness at its root center.

Based on this choice, you associate yourself with a series of pairs of opposites. Thus you either drift aimlessly, or you move resolutely using the Moo Doe moral compass of True/Right/Correct. It is your choice. You either live a life based on excuses, or you learn to improve your life for the better. You either live your life blaming others or circumstances for your misfortunes, or you earn goodness by healing others and serving them. These are choices in life.

Similarly, you can be weighed down in groundless pessimism because of self-doubt, or you can rise joyfully with an active sense of your emerging potential. It is your choice. You can squander your time with false optimism based on wishful thinking, or you can guide yourself with hope and faith based on a certain vision of your future. Again, it is your choice. You can either brandish the selfish power of Doe Chi (disconnected from the source of great natural energy) or use the authentic exercises and movements of Nae Gong to connect with the unlimited energy of nature.

In all of these cases, you can use your freedom of choice to change your reality for the better. Life is not a prison. Life is a challenge for good and for bad, an opportunity to gain balance, harmony, peace, joy, and great external and internal strengths. Life is a time to cultivate the good seeds to pass on to the coming generations as a legacy worth remembering forever.

QUESTIONS FOR DAILY LIVING

These are some questions to help you apply this lesson to your life.

- Why would you seek to blame others when you can have the joy of healing others?
- Why would you imprison yourself when you have the power to set yourself free and, in turn, help free your family, your community, and many others?
- Why would you choose to be alone on the Pa Doe pathway (isolated, alienated from others) when you can be together with loved ones and friends on the Chung Doe pathway?
- Why would you suffer from insecurity and self-doubt when you can rise majestically on the wings of wisdom?
- Why would you be content with limited power when you can enjoy the blessings of unlimited power through Nae Gong?
- Why would you succumb to unfounded pessimism, on the one hand, or shallow optimism,

on the other, when you can move forward with certain hope based on an enlightened vision of your future?

- Why would you tolerate the effects of natural disease when you can be well?
- Why would you abusively shorten your life when you can live to a more venerable age?
- Why would you grow stagnant when you can be continually moving (earning and learning)?
- Why would you choose to become Keum Soo when you can become In Gan?
- Why would you pass on "rotten fruit" as a legacy when you can pass on the good seeds of harmony, balance, service, togetherness, integrity, peace, joy, and great external and internal strengths?

In short, why would you become anything less than your greatest potential? By accepting responsibility for your own progress and learning to change your reality, you become a role model for others. When others see your courage and follow in your footsteps they become companions with you on the Chung Doe pathway, and, together, you and they can grow steadily to attain the highest potential. You have the choice. You can change your reality.

GREAT STRENGTH OF MIND AND BODY IN HARMONY: THAT IS THE BENEFIT OF NAE GONG

奮田發

Do one's best

7

BECOME A LIVING
VESSEL OF WISDOM

THE SEVENTH STEP OF MOO DOE is to achieve mind over matter by becoming a living vessel of wisdom (a practitioner of wisdom) for your own success and for many others. Out of the basic rhythm of human experience emerge two dominant rhythms: the positive one of Chung Doe and the negative one of Pa Doe. The positive rhythm is the upward climb from one mountain to the next toward the light, following True/Right/Correct. The negative rhythm is the downward spiral toward darkness, following the shifting and deceptive values of Gan Sa. Only by learning and sharing wisdom can a human being remain securely on the upward pathway toward In Gan, the highest form of humanness, and leave behind the good seed for coming generations.

- Life on the human pathway (Doe) is a never-ending challenge for good or for bad.
- The victory of Chung Doe over Pa Doe is the victory of mind over matter.
- Winning in life means winning yourself. Winning yourself means winning your mind and body.
- Truth without Correct is poison. Wisdom is the food of enlightenment.
- Gan Sa truth is based on constant flux. Eternal truth is based on principle.
- First fill your cup, then pour. You cannot pour and fill at the same time.
- Once you have balance, then you begin to have light. Once you have light, you become light. Once you become light, you have peace. This is the beginning of true enlightenment.
- The bridge between learning and earning is responsibility.

The Living Vessel

A heavy mist was blanketing the countryside when the student opened his sleepy eyes and rose slowly from his bed before dawn. Too quickly the time for his lesson with the grandmaster was approaching. His body still ached from the hours of intense training the evening before. Truly he felt like staying in bed. But he recalled the grandmaster's parting words: "The victory of Chung Doe over Pa Doe is the victory of mind over matter." Thus, he hurried out the door and groped his way up the trail through the fog.

By the time he reached the grandmaster's cottage, the first rays of dawn were beginning to clear the air. "Perhaps it will be a good day after all," thought the student as he knocked on the door. Moments later the grandmaster appeared.

"Good morning, Grandmaster," the student said, bowing respectfully.

The grandmaster spoke not a word, but looked around as if he did not see anyone at his doorstep.

"Good morning," repeated the student, putting on his broadest grin.

"I hear a voice," said the grandmaster, reaching down to take up a handful of earth, "and I see footprints in the pathway, but there is nothing here but this clay."

"Here I am," objected the student, pointing at himself.

"Body here, maybe," said the grandmaster, "mind not here."

The student lowered his head and said, "I was sore and tired from the practice yesterday. Sleep did not come easily because I was so uncomfortable."

"Did you want to come this morning?" asked the grandmaster.

"Yes, of course," replied the student.

Immediately, the grandmaster frowned and raised a finger.

"Well, the pillow was tempting," quickly confessed the student, "but I am truly happy to be here now."

"Feelings change constantly," replied the grandmaster. "Body sore, body rested; body tired, body fresh; body hungry, body full: many different feelings. If you go by how you feel in any given moment, you will lack focus and direction--like walking through the forest in a dense fog. But when you go by True/Right/Correct, you go by principle, and principle never changes. How do you feel now?"

"I am ready to learn more," declared the student.

The grandmaster smiled and said, "Now your truth changes. Before, you did not want to practice your lesson. Now you do."

"Yes, Grandmaster," admitted the student, following his teacher into the cottage. "Now I am beginning to understand."

The grandmaster placed his handful of clay into the student's hands, which he held in his own and squeezed gently, and said, "Winning in life means winning yourself. Winning yourself means winning your mind and body.

You will mold yourself like this clay. You will learn to make correct decisions no matter what you are feeling at the moment. That will give you strength and peace. Do you see this jar?"

The student fixed his eyes on a beautiful earthen jar placed on a small stand nearby.

"This jar has been passed down over many generations by wise teachers," said the grandmaster. "One day soon it will be yours. It was prepared by skilled hands using just the right mixture of water and clay, just the right heat of the oven, just the right air in cooling. What is this jar used for?"

"To hold grains and fruits," answered the student.

"Yes," replied the grandmaster. "You, too, will be a vessel like this, a living vessel for carrying the good seeds of service and wisdom for the coming generations. But you have much to learn before you can rise up with wisdom. Most importantly, you must learn that truth is poison."

"What do you mean, Grandmaster?" asked the student, shocked.

"If you follow only the truth you feel at the moment," replied the grandmaster, "you are on the downward path of Pa Doe. Truth with feelings without using Correct is the wrong way. That is Gan Sa—endless changing, endless flux. Tell me, is this not poison?"

"Yes," agreed the student.

"But if you act on True and Right by following what is Correct," explained the grandmaster, "you are on the

Chung Doe pathway, the good pathway. Gan Sa truth is based on constant change. Eternal truth is based on never-changing principle. That is wisdom."

"I understand," responded the student. "My truth now makes me want to practice, because it is Correct. It is the good way of Chung Doe."

"That is correct," confirmed the grandmaster. "Mind over matter. Your spirit and mind are learning to control your body and your actions. If you go out and try to confront large animals with laziness and lack of self-control, you will not survive. Pa Doe actions are losing actions. Chung Doe actions are winning actions. Do not forget why you are here. Life is a never-ending challenge, for better or for worse, for good or for bad. That is why you should train your mind and body. Go and practice now, and afterwards come to see me in the Am Ja."

For a while, the student practiced the difficult exercises and movements of his training. "Mind over matter," he kept thinking. "Living vessel of wisdom," he kept saying over and over to himself.

"Leave good seeds behind," he whispered. He felt the rhythm of his movements, and he felt harmony and peace. By the time he was through, his mouth was parched and dry, and his clothing was drenched with perspiration. Then he went to the Am Ja as directed. Drained and thirsty, the student bowed before his teacher. His eyes then caught sight of things on the table: a bowl of water, a dish of mountain vegetables, and a portion of rabbit meat.

With his eyes, the grandmaster directed the student to be seated, and then asked, "Is it really true that you are thirsty?"

"Yes," replied the student.

"Then drink," said the grandmaster. The student eagerly did so.

"Are you still thirsty?" again asked the grandmaster.

"No more," replied the student.

"So your true feeling has changed?" asked the grandmaster.

"It has," confirmed the student.

"Is it true you are hungry?" asked the grandmaster.

The student's eyes returned to the food, and the delicious aroma in the air tickled his nostrils. The grandmaster smiled and said, "Then eat."

Quickly the student overcame his shyness and ate until every morsel was gone. "Are you hungry now?" again asked the grandmaster.

"No, Grandmaster," replied the student.

"No longer hungry, so your truth has changed again," observed the grandmaster. "How do you feel now?" he asked.

The student bowed and patiently waited.

"In our daily life," continued the grandmaster, "feelings change constantly. Thus our truth changes constantly. What is the name for that?"

"Gan Sa," answered the student.

"Yes," said the grandmaster. "Truth from Gan Sa is always changing. Truth from Gan Sa is like dry leaves in autumn--spiraling down and around, carried every which way by the shifting winds. Many times Gan Sa truth is without Correct. If you act upon such truth, thinking it is right, when it is not Correct, you are on the Pa Doe pathway. Thus your actions do not do the most good for the most people. Do you understand?"

"Yes," said the student, "I understand that Correct is based on principle, and principle never changes."

The grandmaster put his arm around his student's shoulder and said, "Come, let us walk to the valley. Perhaps you can add more to your wisdom this day."

"Living vessel of wisdom," thought the student to himself, and he smiled.

Presently they came to a place where the trail divided itself into three pathways, all of them leading down into the valley. "Which path shall we take?" asked the grandmaster.

"I would be pleased to have you choose," replied the student.

"Yesterday we took the path on the right, so today let us follow the one on the left," decided the grandmaster. "What do you see now?"

Thinking for a moment, the student then answered, "Grandmaster, I am beginning to see things more clearly. Gan Sa is always looking for change, variety, something different. That is often no good."

The grandmaster replied, "Yes, Gan Sa is like poison to life. Gan Sa is consumed with itself so much that it blocks the view of the Correct. Gan Sa is matter over mind. Wisdom is mind over matter. Wisdom is the Chung Doe way of balance, service, peace, and joy. Look down there at the valley. What do you see?"

The student saw that the fog was still lingering over the valley and kept silent.

"Up here in the mountain our choices are few," continued the grandmaster. "Down there in the valley the choices are many. That is the realm of Gan Sa. Gan Sa is the realm of confusion and flux. That is why you need practice—mentally and physically. With practice, you win. When you have light and faith, nothing breaks you. With light and faith, you make correct decisions. Thus you become light in your true self. If you are light, there is no darkness, no fear. Nothing can destroy you. How do you feel?"

"Much stronger, Grandmaster!" replied the student.

"When you follow the Chung Doe pathway your light helps others," said the grandmaster. "It is up to them to accept it and learn from it. When they learn, they too become light. Your sharing is your earning, the good seed. What light you pass on to others is the true earning. When you are light, others come to you. You are a living vessel of wisdom, a living vessel of light. Do you understand?"

"Yes, Grandmaster," the student replied, feeling a swelling in his bosom.

The grandmaster finished the lesson with these words: "Light intimidates the night. Light never intimidates those who seek to act with Correct, because that is the way to help others. One must follow the light to become light. Light dispels the fog of Gan Sa. Now, go on from here alone and practice to become light."

"Yes, Grandmaster," said the student, bowing humbly. "I truly look forward to the next lesson, but what is the key to winning mind over matter?"

"One of the ways to win yourself and gain enduring inner strength is Nae Gong," calmly replied the grandmaster. "Tomorrow I will begin to teach you Nae Gong, a way to open up the invisible eye and find the way of success."

THE LESSON

For centuries, practitioners of Moo Doe morals have passed down the master key for achieving and spreading balance, harmony, and peace in a world of flux and turmoil. This master key opens the unlimited reserves of light and energy essential for dispelling the effects of Gan Sa in our world. Gan Sa is the seductive web of change and flux that entices humans to seek ever new and different ways to satisfy their greedy appetites and cater to their shifting selfish feelings. Humans pay allegiance to what they consider True and Right, but often a fickle taskmaster enslaves them. What they consider True and Right, if not guided by Correct, is often nothing but fleeting feelings and emotions. When humans are caught in this web, the result is often anger, jealousy, and divisiveness. Many humans place great value on being "right" and "making their point." This is often the cause of arguments, battles, and even wars. In such an atmosphere, the steady compass of wisdom is rendered inoperative, and is replaced by a compass of shifting values and opinions. How shall the course be followed when the compass changes every moment? How shall the destination be reached when the map changes constantly and there is no direction?

TRUTH IS POISON

Truth is what we sense is real in a given moment. One moment we are thirsty; then after we drink we are satisfied. One moment we are hungry; then after we eat we are filled. One moment we cry; the next we laugh. One moment we are sleepy; then later we are rested. One moment we love; the next we hate.

If we tie our life plan to such shifting truth, we are without an anchor and without direction. Only by aiming for the Correct can we survive. The Correct asks: "What will do the most enduring good for the most human beings? What will bring the most light into the darkness? What will bring the most harmony and peace into a world of chaos? What will bring the most love into a world of hate and anger?" Truth without Correct is a spiral downward into night. Truth with Correct is the climb upward into day. Truth without Correct is poison, but truth with Correct leads to wisdom. Wisdom is the food of enlightenment because it nourishes peace and harmony by pointing everyone to a higher standard of never-changing principle.

When humans act on True and Right without Correct, they may be sincere in their motivation, but sincerity is no protector of principle. All parties to war may be equally sincere, the parties of divorce, the same. When a relationship is strained, all parties may insist that their truth and right are supreme. That may serve to escalate the divisions and engender anger and hate. Who therefore shall bring a change to this cycle? Who shall replace war with peace? Who shall mend the marriage and repair the relationship? Who shall be a role model of integrity and wisdom? Who shall follow principle rather than emotion and transitory need? There is perhaps no greater need in the world today--East, West, North, and South--than the key to governing your actions wisely and correctly by the application of unchanging principle. If you know your (true) self, you are seeking light and wisdom and cultivating the good seed to pass on to coming generations--you become a role model in a world hungry for such role models. When families are guided by such role models, the community is strong. Individuals of light, families of light, communities of light--what more does it take to build harmony, peace, and joy than for each human being to seek to learn and earn wisdom, to seek to cultivate the good seed to pass on to future generations?

MIND OVER MATTER: RHYTHM OF SUCCESS

Life is a never-ending challenge for good or for bad. All life has rhythm. The human way (Doe) is the harmony of coming and going, up and down, and in and out. The experience of life is the balance between joy and sadness, pleasure and pain, health and sickness, and union and separation. What do we learn from all of this ebb and flow? Are we tossed about in the currents of life like foam on the waves? Or do we set our course by the lodestar of principle and extract from our days and years the precious fragments of wisdom that add up to harmony and balance?

There is a rhythm of success and a rhythm of failure. The rhythm of success is an upward climb from one mountain to the next in the direction of the light. The destination is In Gan the highest form of humanness. The compass is the Moo Doe moral compass of True/Right/Correct. The pathway is Chung Doe. The strategy is to learn and earn wisdom through reality. The legacy is to leave behind the good seeds of harmony, balance, peace, joy, and great external and internal strengths. This is mind over matter. This is aligning yourself with destiny and taking control of your progress. This is connecting with the invisible powers of healing.

On the other hand, the rhythm of failure is a downward spiral toward darkness. The destination is Keum Soo, the animal form of humanness with a thousand masks, one for each false identity. The unstable compass is the fleeting truths of the moment, the web of shifting feelings and values called Gan Sa. The pathway is Pa Doe. The strategy is to be right and unique at all costs, to be drunk with abundance and variety at the expense of Correct. The legacy is rotten fruit, good for nothing but to be recycled to the earth. This is not the way of harmony and peace and togetherness. This is the way of isolation and weakness and death. This is matter over mind. This is rebelling against destiny and relinquishing control of your progress. This is destroying the connecting ties to the invisible powers of healing.

These two dominant rhythms emerge out of the basic rhythm of life. These two rhythms offer a grand choice to each human being. Will you follow the rhythm of success or the rhythm of failure--the upward curving steps or the downward spiral? With which one of these two rhythms do you resonate? What is your true nature: to seek mind over matter, or matter over mind?

RESPONSIBILITY

Embarking on the Chung Doe pathway includes a commitment and a promise. The human being commits to discovering his or her own true self and promises to cultivate the good seeds for the coming generations. Learning and earning are the responsibility of the Chung Doe traveler who sets out to achieve success in life. Learning is the accumulation of knowledge. Knowledge is the range of information and understanding about the particular subject. From the vast and complex spectrum of knowledge available in the world, the Chung Doe traveler selects those sources that enlarge the understanding of enduring principles and illuminate the pathway toward In Gan. Like shifting truths, knowledge can be seductive in its endless variety. Thus, the Chung Doe traveler uses True/Right/Correct to select learning that contributes to harmony, balance, peace, and joy and leads to light.

Learning must precede earning. Earning is being the good role model for others, serving their needs, and cultivating the good seeds to leave behind as a legacy. Down through the centuries has come the counsel: learn, then earn. Swallow your food of knowledge before speaking words of wisdom. Fill the cup before pouring. You cannot fill and pour at the same time. Thus, you cannot be filled up and pour out wisdom to others at the same time. Learn, then earn.

The Chung Doe traveler becomes the living vessel of wisdom. Wisdom is the key to the use of the Correct in daily life. Wisdom solves the paradox of shifting truth by coupling True and Right with Correct. Truth has three faces: What we feel at the moment (momentary truth), what we know to be a fact (factual truth), and what we know to be correct (eternal truth, or truth in alignment with unchanging principle). Wisdom clearly distinguishes among these three and points the way to Correct. If we act on momentary truths, thinking that our decisions are right, we are in danger of acting with no connection to the non-changing foundation of principle. But if we look at the patterns of momentary and factual truth, and then seek to do that which is correct (doing the most good for the most human beings), we act on principle. In that way, we combine True (how we feel and what we know to be factual) and Right (our best judgment for action) with Correct (eternal principle). The result is an increase in harmony, peace, and togetherness in our families and communities. This is the way of wisdom.

THE GLUE OF WISDOM

Wisdom allows us to realize that only by following the Correct is the acceptable use of True and Right. Using insight, good sense, and proper judgment, we help others in their search for freedom, health, and balance. We gladly accept the opportunity to serve others because, as Chung Doe travelers, we know it is our responsibility to do so. It is a natural outgrowth of the upward climb toward In Gan, the highest form of humanness. With our invisible eye, we see clearly that our role in life is to become living vessels of wisdom. Our truest feelings are based on a desire to serve. It is also a true fact of our experience that such service to others, if they are accepting, brings them more harmony, peace, joy, and strength. Thus it is Right that we accept this responsibility and act on it, because such action aligns us with eternal principle and thus is Correct.

Becoming a living vessel of wisdom means continually learning and earning. The bridge between learning (acquiring more knowledge) and earning (sharing with others) is responsibility. When we cross this bridge we bring wisdom to others. Wisdom generates peace in a world of anger, joy in a world of sadness, and love in a world of hate. Wisdom is the glue between and among humans, the bond among families and communities. Wisdom is the soap that allows oil and water to mix. Wisdom is "U Hwa," the key to balancing opposites. Our responsibility is to learn and earn wisdom to become light in order to bring balance into life.

Life is a never-ending challenge for good or for bad. It is our wish to choose the good, which leads to freedom, balance, and great inner peace. How does this happen? Once you have balance, then you begin to have light. Once you have light, you become light. Once you become light, you have peace. That is the beginning of true enlightenment (fully balancing oneself--physically, mentally, and spiritually).

GREAT STRENGTH OF MIND AND BODY IN HARMONY: THAT IS THE FRUIT OF WISDOM

精神一到何事不成

Where there
is a will,
there is
a way.

8

DRAW ON NATURE'S POWER THROUGH NAE GONG

THE EIGHTH STEP TO MOO DOE is to align your true self with the natural energy of the universe through the correct use of Nae Gong. Nae Gong means "internal energy"--the limitless dynamic energy that generates, promotes, and sustains all life. The exquisite system of Nae Gong exercises and movements is one of the central ways for opening the invisible eye of the true self and gaining access to extraordinary levels of energy for healing and enlightenment. Through the proper selection of movements and correct touching of the energy points, you can dramatically accelerate the flow of benefits for extending life and increasing vitality. Nae Gong can help you transform the eight steps of *The Master Key of Wisdom* into lasting change to bless the lives of individuals, families, and communities.

- With Nae Gong, there is light.
- Through Nae Gong, you can connect with the natural stream of energy--wind, fire, and water--and promote wellness and great internal and external strengths.
- Touching pressure points accelerates the Nae Gong progress up the Moo Doe mountain in miraculous ways.
- Which of the Nae Gong exercises and movements to use for a given human in a given situation--that is the great mystery that wisdom can solve.
- The modern-day pains of stress, imbalance, anxiety, rapid aging, and lack of energy can be healed through Nae Gong.
- This is the age of integrative healing in which the knowledge of the West and the wisdom of the East are flowing together to enrich and extend life to the fullest.
- Nae Gong makes *The Master Key of Wisdom* an enduring part of your daily life.
- Human beings are waiting for the healing. Learn it, then earn it. Bring it to them. That is the purpose of In Gan—highest form of humanness and humanness at its root center. That is your destiny.

The Day the Grandmaster Spoke No Words

Shortly before dawn, the student walked up to the grandmaster's cottage and found a note pinned to the door. It read: "Meet me at the mouth of the canyon and tell me the answer to this riddle: What has many words, but only one word; many waters, but only one water; many winds, but only one wind; many lights, but only one light?"

Struck with fear at the mystery of this task, the student made his way quickly up the path. Presently he came upon the waterfall cascading over a rocky ledge near the mouth of the canyon. The cool spray felt refreshing on his face. Then he heard the canyon wind rustling through the evergreen trees and felt it blowing through his hair. As he turned the last bend in the trail, the sun rose above the horizon behind him and bathed the valley far below in warmth. He felt that warmth across his shoulders and back.

What did all of this mean—the note, the riddle, the unusual meeting place? He continued up the path until he had climbed above the waterfall. Then he spotted the grandmaster ahead of him, seated on a rock near the stream. The grandmaster motioned for him to sit down nearby.

"Good morning, Grandmaster," said the student, bowing politely.

But the grandmaster only smiled and pointed with his finger to the rising sun.

The student nodded and remarked, "It is a beautiful sunrise."

At that, the grandmaster frowned and kept pointing to the sun, signaling his expectation to hear a better answer.

Near panic, the student thought to himself, "Light, heat, warmth. What should I say?" Then the words of the note came back to him: "Many lights but only one light." Quickly he blurted out, "We are all waiting for the sun."

The grandmaster smiled but kept pointing. "We are all waiting for the sun," repeated the student. "Each has need of the sun. A sun for each. Many suns are needed."

The grandmaster kept smiling, and the student repeated, "Many suns are needed, but we have only one sun. Many lights, but only one light."

The grandmaster smiled, nodded slightly, and raised his hand as if to say, "Enough." Yet, then, he pointed to the stream beside him.

"I see the stream has divided itself into many channels," said the student. Then, he had an insight and exclaimed, "Many waters but only one water!"

The grandmaster smiled and pointed to a section of the stream that had spread out into a shallow pond, separated from the main flow of water and held back by a ridge of earth. The water in the pond was murky and stagnant. The grandmaster reached out and scraped away the earthen barricade. Immediately the water in the little pond broke through and rejoined the main stream, which flowed on down toward the waterfall.

The grandmaster raised an eyebrow, and the student said, "Well, I believe the motion of the water serves to purify the stream. The trapped water has now been purified."

The grandmaster nodded in approval, then reached down and plucked a seed cluster from a nearby plant. He shook it first above his head, then to his right side, then to his left. Each time a gust of wind carried the seedlings to a different location.

"Many winds," said the student without prompting, "but only one wind."

At this, the grandmaster nodded his approval, then preceded to do something extraordinary, the likes of which the student had never before seen. Pushing his small wicker basket to one side of the rock, the grandmaster stood up and performed a series of exquisite patterns and movements with his body and limbs. The student watched spellbound as this display of precise and beautiful artistry continued for many minutes. A feeling of awe overcame the student as he felt within himself a sense of being in the presence of great power. Not unlike the sensation produced by the sun and the wind and the waterfall, the sensation of deep reverence awakened by this experience, lifted the student's spirits and buoyed his hope that one day he too could learn this exquisite movement.

After the grandmaster finished his movements, he returned to his rocky perch. He, then, raised his eyebrow but the student did not know what to say. The grandmaster pointed to the sun, then the stream, and then passed his hand quickly through the air. Following that he held up four fingers.

Immediately the student understood that he was to consider the fourth and missing part of the riddle, "What has many words, but only one word?" His mind raced over all the possibilities relating to the movements he had seen, but he could think of nothing to say.

It did not help that the grandmaster was frowning, and the student was simply lost for words. The grandmaster stared at him in silence for what seemed like a long while. Then, he reached over and opened the wicker basket next to him. He gently took out a small bird that quivered weakly in his hand, clearly suffering from some form of illness.

The student watched in rapt silence as the grandmaster reached down and drew some water from the stream and tenderly moistened the head of the bird. He held the bird so that the rays of the sun warmed its feathers, and he blew gently over its weakened body. Then, he held the bird in his cupped hands so that only its tail feathers could be seen. After a few moments, he closed his eyes and concentrated a long while.

The student dared not breathe or make a sound. Presently the grandmaster opened his eyes and held his arms toward the sun. When he opened his hands, an extraordinary thing occurred. The bird shook its head vigorously, chirped, spread its wings, and flew with a gust of wind over the stream and directly toward the sun, until it had disappeared from view.

The student was speechless. He looked over at the grandmaster, who smiled and raised his eyebrows. The student could think of nothing adequate to say. The grandmaster shook his head sternly from side to side. Then he pointed back down the pathway, a signal for the student to leave.

"What has many words, but only one word?" thought the student to himself as he humbly bowed to the grandmaster and started back down the trail. "I shall have to find the answer by tomorrow," whispered the student to himself, disappointed.

The next morning the student approached the grandmaster's cottage with a sense of concern. He had devised many answers to the riddle, but none of them seemed correct. The student began to wonder, how would the grandmaster respond? The last time such a thing had happened, the grandmaster had made him sit alone for many hours until he had come up with the answer.

The door opened and the grandmaster appeared. "Good morning, Grandmaster," said the student.

"Good morning," responded the grandmaster, much to the student's relief. "I see from your eyes that you do not yet understand. Come in."

The student entered the cottage and took a seat in the corner as directed. He was breathing nervously.

"You may be at ease," said the grandmaster. "What you saw yesterday has been passed down over time for many centuries, many generations. It is the key for connecting with great natural energy."

"Nae Gong," hesitantly whispered the student.

"Yes," replied the grandmaster, "hold out your hand." The student instantly obeyed.

The grandmaster dipped a small sponge in a bowl of water and held it above the student's palm. "Count," he said.

The student counted each drop as it fell into the palm of his hand. "One, two, three, four," he said, continuing until he reached ten.

"How many drops?" asked the grandmaster.

"Te...," began the student yet suddenly said, "One!"

The grandmaster smiled and said: "All water is one. The drops separate, but they flow back together. There is great energy in water. Nature has a magnificent circulation system. You can feel the dew on the grass. You can see the stream. The rains bring waters from the heavens. That is the way of nature's power. Your body, too, has a magnificent circulation system for nourishing and cleansing itself. The Nae Gong movements enhance this system in wonderful ways. That is the principle. What is the closest invisible thing touchable to you right now?"

The student became flushed. The grandmaster reached over and took the student's hand, passing it quickly through the air.

"Air," replied the student. "Invisible, but I can feel it."

"Yes," confirmed the grandmaster, "how you breathe is a key to well-being. The Nae Gong movements enhance the vital cleansing process of breathing. That is the principle. What do you feel?" The grandmaster held his palm out in front of himself, toward the student.

"I feel the heat, Grandmaster. Like fire," replied the student, stunted.

The grandmaster nodded and said: "Wind, water, and fire are all one (existence, energies) in nature. The heat of the body regulates vitality. The movements of Nae Gong enhance the process and balance these three aspects of natural energy in the body. Through Nae Gong you can Connect with this natural stream of energy and produce wellness and great internal strength. What has many words, but only one word?"

The student sat up straight in his seat and thought to himself, "The riddle!" He was baffled and still did not know how to answer it. Hence the grandmaster continued, "Over the centuries the grandmasters have cultivated and passed down the Nae Gong movements to the coming generations. There are many thousands of movements. But which one produces the correct result for a given human in a given circumstance? That is the wisdom of the ages. Many movements, but only one movement. Many thousands of names, but only one that is correct."

"Many words, but only one word," said the student, his eyes lighting up.

"You are beginning to understand," replied the grandmaster. "With the invisible eye you, will learn to understand without using words. With the invisible tongue, you will be able to make yourself understood without speaking. Wisdom has a language all its own. Many words, but only one word. What is the word?"

Still uncertain of the answer, the student did not say anything.

"Think of the bird," said the grandmaster.

"Healing," hesitantly replied the student.

"Yes," said the grandmaster. "All life is a never-ending challenge for good or for bad. Choose the good. Choose the way of healing. Pass the good seeds on to your children and the coming generations. They are waiting for the sun. They are waiting for the wind. They are waiting for the water. Fire, wind, water--these are all one (coming from one source). It is healing. They are waiting for that healing. Learn it, then earn it. Bring it to them. That is your destiny."

The student felt a great sense of purpose, a great sense of mission. "How shall I bring all these things together as one and learn to heal?" he asked.

"The fire is the heat of your body balanced by practicing special movements," explained the grandmaster. "Secret herbal tea formulas balance your blood, which is the water. The wind, your breath, is balanced using proper breathing and meditation techniques. Through research over the centuries, this combination has been used to bring nature's energy into your body. You must learn to unite all three, the special movements, herbal tea formulas, with breathing and meditation, to become one (existence, energy) with nature, harmonious and completely balanced. Internally, meld nature's energy with your own to develop tremendous internal strength. Once achieved you can live your life to the fullest. That is the lesson for life."

THE LESSON

Over the centuries, those who have practiced Moo Doe at the highest levels of accomplishment have developed a powerful system for enhancing health and vitality in extraordinary ways. The virtually limitless energy of nature--exhibited in the forces of fire, wind, and water--can be channeled to any human being who knows the way to become connected with it. The master key for that kind of connection is the correct practice of Nae Gong, a magnificent system of movements and breathing exercises that has emerged over the centuries. The definitive form of Nae Gong became standardized a few centuries ago and has changed very little since then. Only a small number of humans in the world today understand and practice Nae Gong in its proper execution, with its full range of benefits. Those who do are aware that human life can be extended significantly and the effects of natural infirmities eased or eliminated by using the ancient patterns of movement, moving meditation, and Nae Gong in correct ways over time.

Practitioners of Nae Gong deeply sense the responsibility to share this kind of wisdom with others, thus leaving behind a legacy of good seeds for the coming generations. In the past, certain qualified humans were selected to receive this kind of training, based primarily on their qualities of integrity, honor, and character. In truth, not all humans are prepared to understand and receive such wisdom. Thus, the number of recipients over time has been rather small--until now.

Throughout the centuries, Moo Doe practice has always been total and complete in its methodology. This development begins with its most basic steps, which systematically progress and mature into more intricate patterns, each demanding more focus and devotion. As each level is attained, advancement in rank is reached and certification duly noted.

NAE GONG AS THE PEAK OF A MOUNTAIN

If you think of a mountain as the symbol for advancement toward knowledge of the true self and a state of greater vitality, balance, and strength, then the climb upward can be divided into three main levels of progress.

Level I: The foothills, consisting of Myung Sang (Chi Gong), are a select series of eight different sets of meditation exercises that establish the foundation for obtaining greater harmony, balance, and well-being in daily living.

Level II: The mountain, which is above these foothills and is rising in majesty with U Dong Myung Sang, is a select series of 18 different sets of "moving meditation" exercises that enhance the effects of the training and bring the practitioner dramatically closer to the goal of alignment with natural energies.

Level III: The summit, which is above the middle level of the mountain, is the pinnacle of mind and body balance, internal and external harmonization, and greatly increased strength. Encompassed at this highest level are the first 36 different selected sets of Nae Gong exercises for maximum strength and development. This peak level of progress embraces a carefully formulated sequence of exquisite and beautiful movements that are designed to channel the maximum benefit to the practitioner. Nae Gong means "internal energy" and is one of the central methodologies for opening up the "invisible," "spiritual" eye of the true self and giving the mind and body access to sources of remarkable natural energy for healing and enlightenment.

ACCELERATING THE CLIMB

In traditional approaches to Moo Doe training the pace of progress is deliberate, requiring much patience and endurance. Climbing just the foothills of Myung Sang successfully sometimes requires years to complete. However, there is a "key" that can accelerate the progress up the mountain. That "key," in some cases, involves touch—the correct touching of certain vital energy points by the practitioner during the exercises for the purpose of opening the energy lines (Hyuel). When this is done with precision and exactness, the climb up the mountain of mind and body mastery and enlightenment is reduced to a fraction of the normal time. Patience and focus remain indispensable, but the results can come more quickly. In addition, those who have mastered these techniques know how to discern which of them are most beneficial for a given body type and a given set of needs. This mastery of selection is an added factor in accelerating the speed of deriving the powerful benefits from Nae Gong. In fact, depending on the practitioner, significant benefits can be felt quickly, and many lasting results obtained in as little as months, weeks, or days. The key is the selection of exercise and movement techniques, the strategic touch points, and the follow-through and discipline of the practitioner.

NATURE'S SILENT REMEDY

One other vital aspect of correct Nae Gong practice must be mentioned. Over the centuries, grandmasters of the healing arts have invariably combined touch, meditation, moving meditation, and Nae Gong movements with the correct administering of natural herbs. The knowledge of precisely which herbs to use in connection with which circumstances and needs is a central element of the highly protected tradition of proven methods for enhancing well-being and vitality passed down through the generations of the royal lines. Herbs are generally classified in three groups according to the benefits they can bring to the upper, middle, and lower sections of the body in response to symptoms and desired outcomes. The use of nature's "silent remedy"— with correct selection, preparation, amounts, timing, frequency, and means of application (usually in the form of herbal teas, but also sometimes as incense or vapors) provides an extraordinary supplement to the Nae Gong benefits. The time has come to share with a wider audience, key elements of this highly effective system for achieving balance of mind and body by correctly utilizing nature's vast storehouse of life-sustaining and health-preserving plants and herbs.

THE BENEFITS OF NAE GONG

The human mind and body entity exists as part of nature and participates in the interplay of natural energies. There is an analogue relationship between the systems of nature and the systems of the body. The three points of concurrence are wind, fire, and water. Wind relates to the body's respiratory system—the air we take into our body to sustain life. Fire relates to the temperature of the body and the critical role it plays in all functions of life. Water relates to the body's circulatory system, essential for vitality and well-being. Nae Gong exercises and movements deeply affect all organs, joints, and muscles. After all, Nae Gong is the internal energy that constitutes the life of the human being. Without Nae Gong, there is no life. When properly used, the Nae Gong exercises and movements greatly increase flexibility, speed, and coordination, and produce tremendous strength—a lifetime benefit.

Nae Gong is one of the principal avenues for accessing the limitless reserve of natural energy that pervades our world and sustains all life. By working with nature through Nae Gong, the practitioner can bring about incredible internal and external strengths. In addition, when these strengths are combined with the Nae Gong system for achieving great balance and harmony, the single force of energy produces a miraculous upsurge in the vital forces of health and well-being in the human being. The modern-day pains of stress, imbalance, anxiety, accelerated aging, and lack of energy can be healed by the natural and exquisite movements of Nae Gong. In addition, those who have mastered the exercise and movement techniques can acquire the increased energy to strengthen and heal specific areas of the body, both for themselves as well as for others.

VITAL QUESTIONS

Why should a human being not have the life of quality and well-being? Why should human life not extend naturally to 100 years and longer since it is biologically proven possible? Why should we not be able to control natural illnesses with greater facility? With such enormous natural stores of energy all around us in the universe, why should we not be able to tap into them readily for the blessing of individuals, families, and communities? Why should we not be able to conquer debilitating stress and imbalances in our modern world using natural exercises and movements?

The answer to these questions is of interest to every human being. Nae Gong is the answer, because it is one of the most important ways to "quality life," extend life, increase energy, reduce stress, overcome many kinds of natural ailments, and improve the ability of the mind and body to prevent the onset of disease. Nae Gong also facilitates clear thinking, correct decision-making, and cultivating a higher perspective on the values that make life worthwhile by leaving the good seeds--service, integrity, togetherness, respect, honor, and passing on an enduring legacy for the coming generations.

A kind Providence has placed along the pathway of life devoted master teachers with the wisdom and the resolve to make the benefits of Nae Gong available to all who are willing to rise to the challenge of learning and earning (sharing) these great secrets.

THE MASTER KEY TO WISDOM

This is the age in which the knowledge of the West and the wisdom of the East are flowing together to open up enormous opportunities for living life to the fullest. Modern science is beginning to validate the benefits of the age-old wisdom of the Moo Doe grandmasters. More and more respectable schools and professions (particularly medical) in the West are beginning to incorporate elements of Eastern practice into their curricula and plan. Meditation and other alternative approaches are starting to supplement and even supplant current therapies for dealing with the overpowering challenges of modern life. The 21st century will be the age of integrative healing. All of the wisdom and knowledge of the past are beginning to coalesce into a grand whole that is greater than its parts, and holds out the promise of bringing great benefits to those who are willing to participate.

How can you take advantage of this singularly significant point in time? This book has laid out the fundamental insights of age-old secrets for attaining and maintaining a more productive and balanced life. The ideas are simple, but the application is not so simple.

These eight steps combined into a system of Moo Doe moral principles shall provide you tremendous rewards in harmony and well-being.

1. Know your "true" self.
2. Choose the Correct.
3. Overcome Doe Chi.
4. Leave behind the good seeds.
5. Seek the face of honor.
6. Change your reality.
7. Become a living vessel of wisdom.
8. Work with nature through Nae Gong.

How Can You Make This Work for You?

How shall these proven insights and techniques take root in your life? How can you internalize this wisdom and make it an enduring part of your daily routines? How can you ensure that these benefits will flow to you forever with no lessening of effect over time, no forgetting of techniques, nor erosion of the good results?

The answers to these questions are contained in *The Master Key of Wisdom* itself, for the role of rooting this wisdom in your true self is assigned to Nae Gong. These are the principles of Nae Gong.

- With Nae Gong, you can open the invisible (spiritual) eye to learn your true self.
- With Nae Gong, you will be able to choose the Correct on a daily basis.
- With Nae Gong, you will overcome Doe Chi.
- With Nae Gong, you will learn to cultivate the good seeds to leave behind for your family and the coming generations: the good seeds of harmony, balance, peace, joy, and great internal and external strengths.
- With Nae Gong, you will be able to seek the face of honor and abandon all the masks of false identity and false pride.
- With Nae Gong, you will be able to change your reality as you go from challenge to challenge.
- With Nae Gong, you will learn to become a living vessel of wisdom for the benefit of yourself, your family, and your community.
- With Nae Gong, you will be able to work with nature to achieve harmony and vitality, changing your reality for a balanced and better quality of life.

Nae Gong will transform the words of this book into wisdom--an enduring legacy of health and abundance for you and your loved ones. Life is a never-ending challenge for good or for bad. Therefore, choose the good--the Chung Doe pathway. Set your course inexorably toward In Gan, the highest form of humanness. Use Nae Gong to make it last for a lifetime and beyond.

The eight steps of Moo Doe morals outlined in this book constitute a blueprint for achieving harmony, balance, joy, peace, and great strength. Learn, and then earn. Be a light to others. This material, provided here for the first time by a true Moo Doe grandmaster, is a moral program for leaving behind the good seeds for your family and the coming generations. And that is, after all, the purpose of life. Today, that is the destiny with which we choose to align ourselves. The destiny to leave good seeds for a better tomorrow. That is the Chung Doe way. That is your destiny with your "master key" of wisdom.

GREAT STRENGTH OF MIND AND BODY IN HARMONY: THAT IS OUTCOME OF NAE GONG

Epilogue

Peace in a Gan Sa World of Flux and Confusion

So many human beings are looking for peace in today's turmoil--laden world. Why? In this world where daily actions seem to be fueled and controlled by the spirit of Gan Sa--the perpetual quest for variety and change for its own sake--it would seem that peace is the constant that the unsettled human being would seek.

It is the principle of the Chung Doe pathway that choosing the correct way in daily life leads to greater harmony, balance, joy, and peace. Peace comes through being led spiritually. Spiritual peace has its source in the universal Supreme Being. Peace is the clear, smooth way for us in life. With peace, we are not swayed or led astray by others or by our own still-learning selves.

Remember, Gan Sa is enticing and pleasurable only in the beginning. Gan Sa excitement lasts only a short time. It is temporary. Peace lasts forever.

Spiritual peace comes from the greatest entity—the nature of God. Through peace comes happiness. The way to reach this happiness is to choose to follow the Chung Doe pathway. Before human beings, the Chung Doe pathway was there. It is the way to enlightenment—highest spiritual understanding and connection.

The following concluding dialogue is an afterward to this book, and a bridge to the next one.

The End To A Beginning

Near the village was a peaceful wooded hill accessible by a narrow footbridge spanning a small stream. It was on this bridge that the student was to meet the grandmaster before dawn.

"Good morning," said the grandmaster as the student arrived.

"Good morning, Grandmaster," replied the young man, bowing in respect.

The grandmaster nodded. He was standing near the handrail, looking off into the distance. "What do you see down there in the village?" he asked.

"Many people are getting ready for the day," observed the student.

"What are they doing?" asked the grandmaster.

"They are eating breakfast, washing, getting their children off to school, setting up their booths in the market square—many different things."

"How peaceful," commented the grandmaster.

"Peaceful?" remarked the student. "Everything is a beehive of activity!"

"And what are they looking forward to?" asked the grandmaster.

The student stroked his chin and said, "I suppose they are looking forward to the end of the day."

"Why?" asked the grandmaster.

"So they can have rest," said the student.

"And?" further asked the grandmaster.

"Peace," added the student.

"Yes," responded the grandmaster. "Every human being has peace locked inside, waiting to emerge. Why do you suppose you want peace?"

The student pondered for a moment, but could think of no answer to this deep question. Presently a swan glided down the slow-moving side of the stream pursued by several cygnets. "Who is guiding those cygnets?" asked the grandmaster.

"Their mother," responded the student.

"And those people down there in the village, who is guiding them? Who is telling them to eat and wash and prepare and work?" asked the grandmaster.

"Well, no one," said the student. "They are just telling themselves."

"With the mind as their guide," replied the grandmaster, "it is no wonder they are seeking peace. Look there at the surface of the stream. Sometimes a leaf floats down, sometimes a petal, sometimes an insect, sometimes a branch, sometimes a seed. The mind is like that. Left to itself, the mind is forever changing. Thoughts that float through the mind vary by what people see. Is there anything in all of nature that is as changing as the mind? What is the first thing I said to you as you arrived?"

The student was shocked by these words, and struggled to remember. "I believe 'Good morning,'" he replied.

"Good morning, good night, good morning, good night," said the grandmaster. "Why do we seek peace?

Why do we seek enlightenment? Morning and evening, day and night, the endless cycle of life, Yin and Yang. Who guides us at night?"

Again the student was taken by surprise. The grandmaster raised his eyebrows in anticipation of the answer.

"God," said the student.

"Yes," confirmed the grandmaster. "When God leads, there is peace and well-being. But when we let the mind lead, without enlightenment, there is confusion, disorder. The hunger for peace is the hunger for spiritual enlightenment. Locked inside every human being is the seed of peace. But that seed can sprout and grow only in a spiritual light. Who will show the way to that light?"

The student diligently searched for an answer, but had no answer.

The grandmaster smiled and put his arm around the young man, and said: "This bridge leads from the peaceful hillside to the busy village. Many down there have not yet found peace. You are the bridge for them. You are the messenger of hope and peace. You are the vessel of wisdom. You are the guide on the Chung Doe pathway. Help them satisfy their hunger for peace. With spiritual enlightenment, nothing can destroy their peace. With such enlightenment, their happiness is constant— no matter what happens. Thus they will have peace not just at night when they sleep in God, but always and forever. That is the mystery they are waiting to learn."

The student stood straight and tall with honor and confidence, and asked, "Grandmaster, how can I become more like you?"

"Learn, then earn," replied the grandmaster. "Now go in peace and show them the way. Soon we shall meet again."

At that moment, the sun rose and the student began his next journey toward the Chung Doe pathway.

Over the centuries many well-respected, prominent human beings have used *The Master Key of Wisdom* to overcome the challenges of daily life. You have the choice to follow your pathway—Chung Doe or Pa Doe. You can change your reality. That is your destiny. Now you hold in your hand the master key.

GLOSSARY

Am Ja A secluded place of meditation for enlightenment (e.g., a facility in the mountain)

Cheo Syeh Using flattery for personal benefit.

Chung Doe Correct path; good principle; good seed (following good principle); having interest not only in oneself, but also greater interest in others.

Doe Path or way; the human pathway.

Doe Chi (pronounced as Doe Chee) Drunk on one's (your) own thoughts; only believe in what the individual wants to believe (overwhelmingly stubborn and fooling oneself); making choices for only personal gain (selfishness and greediness); doesn't follow good principle (Pa Doe pathway).

Gan Sa Constant change (like the wind that is constantly changing direction) living for the moment, for self gain.

In Gan (pronounced as Een Gan) Highest form of humanness; humanness at its root center; words and actions are one (consistency between your words and actions); to follow the Chung Doe path guided by good principle that is not influenced by pain or adversity.

Hyuel Meridian lines; energy lines; energy channels.

Keum Soo Animal form of humanness; having many faces; a different face for each event; an appearance of human with animal ways, which are out of control and beastly.

Moo Doe A traditional martial arts that follows the Chung Doe way of good principle and value.

Myung Sang A form of Chi Gong (pronounced as Chee Gong) meditation with special breathing techniques.

Nae Gong Natural universal energies (chi: pronounced as chee) stored within special areas of the body (abdomen), which can be attained by special exercises and movements.

Pa Doe Wrong path; bad principle; bad seed (following of bad principle); having selfish interest.

Seok Eun Qua Eel Rotten fruit (lacking morals); bad seeds (Pa Doe pathway).

U Dong Myung Sang Moving meditation balanced with special breathing.

U Hwa Balancing opposites; bringing opposites together into one.

Wae Gong External and internal energy; energy of the mind and body.

Printed in the United States
202315BV00001B/1-51/A

9 781425 993559